The Trouble Maker

For my dear wife and son (Imogen & Cameron),

My brothers (Iradj & Touradj)

&

In loving memory of

Mum & Dad

The Trouble Maker

A colourful memoir "well-seasoned" with

Persian spices

Mike Payami

Acknowledgements

I'd like to express my thanks to my dear wife Imogen and son Cameron for their invaluable help and support.

I'm very lucky to have a wonderful circle of friends and I'd like to thank all of them for the roles they've played in my life's adventures so far!

I'm especially grateful to my wonderful friends Nicky & Denise for their inspiration and structural editing; highlighting both the strengths and weaknesses of my initial draft.

I am also indebted to my good fellow food enthusiast and good cook Chris H for his invaluable assistance, especially his IT help and for being a truly supportive friend during some very hard times.

Lastly, I'm grateful to my wonderful mother for inspiring me with her fabulous food and to my father for teaching me discipline. From them I learnt that my cup is always half full.

Mehrdad (Mike) Payami

April 2018

The Trouble Maker

By Mike Payami

Contents

CHAPTER 1

Sabzee Polo Mahee & Fish and Chips

At about 12 noon on 7th August 1974, a Boeing 747 jumbo jet with over 400 passengers on board, mainly Iranian teenagers on student visas, touched down on Terminal 2's runway at London's Heathrow Airport. I had no memories of ever flying before and was expecting the landing to involve a great bump and squealing of tyres, but the huge jumbo landed as smoothly as a Swan landing on water.

Picture me at 18. I was wearing a pair of light blue, tight, flared trousers with a rather high, narrow, 30-inch waist (now the stuff of dreams), with the wide band above the zip secured by three buttons. In the front pocket I had a £5 note, and in one of the back pockets carefully stitched up by mother, £100 in brand new banknotes securely tucked away.

A shiny dark brown fake leather aviator jacket, with beige fake fur lapels and an ochre coloured woollen polo neck sweater, with a Fisherman's Cable pattern on the front, completed my fashionable Middle Eastern appearance. Trendy 70's wear at its best!

My long, shiny dark brown hair (again now the stuff of dreams) hung to my shoulders and framed a full beard. I suppose I was trying to look like George Best. The majority of the older students on the plane, who were returning to the UK after spending their summer holiday with their families in Iran, were clean-shaven, so the George Best look was obviously not very popular in the UK. The beard would have to go.

I could only speak very broken English and had heard very little about the Great Britain I was heading towards. I knew about HM the Queen, the Prime Minister of the time, Harold Wilson, and of course, I'd heard of George Best! I knew the names of several London landmarks such as Harrods, Soho, Oxford Street, Hyde Park and the Playboy Club, and I knew that the River Thames, a tidal river, meandered through the city. In addition, of course, like many other Iranian teenagers, I also knew about Top of the Pops and that the Three Degrees' single 'When Will I See You Again', was number one in the charts that week!

From watching many old black and white British films, I had a vision of London being covered for much of the time in a dense 'pea-souper' black fog, so thick that you wouldn't even recognise your own brother at five paces! I thought all the streets were cobbled and lit with the eerie glow of gas lights. Clearly I had watched far too many Dracula or Jack the Ripper films, and for certain, Christopher Lee's infamous toothy grin was an iconic image of my childhood.

I had little idea as to what the food would be like in England, although I knew that fish and chips was a 'national dish'. My last meal in Iran had been a fish dish - *Sabzee Polo Mahee*. This was and still is one of my favourite meals and I'd asked my mother especially for it on the evening before my flight, knowing that I would have to wait nine months or so before I'd be able to share it with my family again around the table.

Apart from in the northern and southern coastal regions, fish (*Mahee*) was fairly expensive to buy in Iran, especially fresh fish. Cooking *Sabzee Polo Mahee* was therefore only affordable for the middle and upper class families. It is traditionally eaten on the Iranian New Year, 'Nowruz'. The *Sabzee Polo* part is a mixture of fluffy steamed rice and green herbs such as coriander, dill, chives, spring onions, fenugreek and parsley. In common with much of Iranian cuisine, this is a very healthy dish, especially if it's prepared with fresh ingredients. For a cheaper and more everyday dish, the fish can be substituted by any type of omelette or frittata, or indeed by the popular Persian herb frittata known as *Koo Koo Sabzee* (see Chpt.8).

The history of Persian (Iranian) cooking goes back to the sixth century B.C., when Cyrus the Great (*Korosh shah*), formed an empire that stretched from India to Egypt, which also included parts of Greece. One can easily recognise Persian food by its wealth of mouth-watering aromas, delicate, well balanced mild flavours and delightful textures. Rice in Iranian cuisine is like pasta in Italy's diet. Iranians without doubt are known to be the masters of fine rice making. Cooking rice Persian style (*Chelow & Polo*) and other accompaniments, is not hard but you may need a few attempts in order to get it right.

My mother's *Sabzee Polo Mahee* dish and a number of tasty side dishes were shared with members of the family, including my granddad (mum's father, whom I adored), the night before my departure to the UK. It was obviously a very special occasion, because I was heading to Europe to become an engineer, with the intention of returning home with all the necessary knowledge and skills, to serve my beautiful country.

The next morning my parents bade me a tearful farewell at Mehrabad International Airport. Iran Air didn't have any jumbo jets in its fleet in 1974, and the particular Boeing I flew on was leased to them by Pan Am. Of course the 747 is now rather an old aircraft and we would barely notice if one flew overhead, but for an 18 year old at that time, it was something quite amazing. The sheer number of passengers, its enormous size, its majestic appearance and its double deck configuration; I remember when I first saw the plane my jaw dropped.

I had a window seat, so as the plane took off I was hoping for a bird's eye view of the beautiful mountain range to the north of Tehran, and a last look at familiar land marks, but unfortunately dawn had not yet broken and all I could see were the shimmering lights of the city growing smaller and smaller, like stars against the blackness as the plane lifted away.

However, being a red blooded Iranian male, I soon forgot my homesickness and transferred my attention to a number of very attractive, friendly, and mainly English air hostesses. I'm sure they must have wondered if I suffered from some kind of metabolic condition, as I asked for snacks and refreshments with such frequency. The six hour flight seemed to pass in no time, so busy had I been with my thoughts of what lay ahead and with my efforts to engage the attention of the air crew.

When the captain asked us to fasten our seat belts in preparation for landing, we were still flying high above the clouds so from the window it was sunny and the sky was clear. Suddenly, the sunlight disappeared as the plane rapidly dipped into dense layers of charcoal grey clouds, which I assumed was the expected London fog! However, we soon passed through the clouds and a bird's eye view of London unfolded beneath me. It took my breath away, and for a few moments I forgot about the existence of the lovely air hostesses.

My first view of London was of the beautiful terracotta colour pitched roofs of the Victorian buildings in Knightsbridge. I saw Harrods and the adjacent lush green Hyde Park, as we swung in on the approach to Heathrow Airport. Unlike the scenes so familiar to me from the films I'd watched, there was no sign of fog beneath us, everything was crystal clear.

I was just getting over the experience of landing when something outside my window distracted me. The plane had taxied for what seemed like miles, and indeed probably was miles, and had now come to a halt next to what had the appearance of a long UFO. Somebody with a rather loud and husky voice said "look, there's a supersonic Concorde next to our plane". Later on I discovered that this Concorde was being prepared for its first test flight to Tehran and then to Bahrain on that very day.

As the other passengers jostled one another in the aisle, I stayed in my seat, determined to be the last to leave. Since I realised that my English chat-up lines were non-existent , I didn't even dare to try to arrange a further meeting with any of hostesses, but just before leaving I did ask the one I fancied most to give me a glass of water. What a plonker! I sipped the water drop by drop for several minutes until the glass was completely empty, then thanked her and left the plane along with its lovely hostesses with some reluctance; entering into yet another very important chapter of my life.

The huge open plan of the arrival section of the terminal building was fascinating and very welcoming. However, the endless queue lines in front of the passport and immigration control desks and the rather hostile questioning by the passport controller, made me feel a little bit like a criminal, and somewhat dimmed the happy feelings within me. After over two hours in the terminal building, it was a relief to see the familiar smiling face of my cousin Manochehre, who was waiting for me outside. He was, like myself, on a student visa but at that time had been living in London for a few years, so his presence, on my first day, in a foreign land was very reassuring for me.

We caught a coach to Victoria Station, and because my final destination from Victoria was only a short train ride away in the suburbs south of London, and the fact that my cousin was unable to accompany me for the complete journey until the following day, I ignored his advice to check into a hotel there, as I was very eager to get to where my college and my future lay as soon as possible.

I reached Tulse Hill after only a few stops. Outside the railway station, there were two very friendly looking young teenagers, who seemed to be almost expecting me. The sight of my large and cumbersome suitcase brought a big smile to their faces. Initially I didn't trust them. I was worried that they might snatch my suitcase and run away with it, but very soon I found out that this was a great opportunity for them. As it turned out, John and Ben earnt some extra pocket money every August and September by showing new students the way to the college, and helping them with their cases. They very politely asked if I was going to South London Technical College and I nodded. They jointly carried my suitcase all the way for nearly two miles and the change I had in my pocket, became lighter by only 50 pence.

The acceptance letter from the college had advised that in order to find suitable long term lodgings, I should report to the accommodation office upon arrival. The secretary at the office, Mrs O'Shea, was a plump and comfortably friendly lady with a gentle Irish burr. After introducing herself and struggling to pronounce my name (Payami, like salami), she asked if I would like to stay temporarily in a youth hostel. Not knowing the meaning of 'hostel', I nodded. I assumed she had guessed that my English wasn't good, because she then asked me about staying in a hall of residence. I didn't know the meaning of 'hall of residence' either so I again nodded hopefully. She then said "I think staying with a good English family would suit you best and it would help you to learn English much faster". Unsure of what she meant, but feeling that a more positive response was called for, I replied 'Maybe'. My answer amused her very much and she told me that from then on she would call me Mr Maybe.

This amusement was shared with another student in the room. She was British, and, it had not escaped my young man's eye, a very pretty petite blonde. We actually became firm friends and through her I later made many more friends at the college. She however, had been amused at my nods of misunderstanding to Mrs O'Shea and as a result nicknamed me Noddy. The name stuck!

Mrs O'Shea managed to make me understand that she knew a very good family who had a room to let to students on a full board basis. They were on holiday at the time, so couldn't send me there directly, but told me that I shouldn't rush into looking for somewhere else, and to wait for this particular family who she felt would really help me settle into my new life. In the meantime she advised I find temporary lodging in a nearby hotel.

With this in mind I left the building and was delighted to see John & Ben again with their friendly grins waiting just outside. They asked me where I would like to go and again carried my suitcase between them for another couple of miles, this time to a very small but comfortable hotel. In those days average house price was just over 11000 pounds, petrol was 11 pence per litre, average full time weekly wage was about 32 pounds and a pack of 20 cigarettes I seem to recall was only 25 pence, so their earnings were extremely good for the eight weeks or so before the start of the academic year.

On the way to the hotel, the inviting smell of a passer-by's chips, wrapped in paper enticed me into a fish and chip shop. It was now 5pm on my first day; my stomach was rumbling and I realised that I'd had nothing to eat since my very early breakfast on the plane. A tasty piece of fish, moist inside and crispy on the outside, and a large portion of chips disappeared with indecent speed. Fried fresh fish in Iran smells appetizing and pleasantly fishy, but this was almost odourless. But I do remember that all the rooms in our home would smell for many days after Mum had fried fish, so maybe it was no bad thing.

My portion of fish and chips together with two extra portions of chips for my helpful luggage carriers cost me about 40 pence, however, by the time I'd bought three cans of coke and paid John & Ben their well-deserved fee , there was still some change left in my front pocket.

The hotel itself and its only vacant room were small but comfortable. Although, to use a lovely English phrase, you couldn't swing a cat in the bedroom; the bathroom was of a relatively good size and contained a sizeable sunken bath. Having spent most of the previous night waiting for my flight in Tehran airport, the long full day I had just experienced was catching up with me. I lay whale-like for half an hour in the sunken bath before tucking myself into bed, under the warm duvet.

I was happy that on my first day in a foreign land everything seemed to have gone so well. Although I had been told that after a while I would be homesick, as an 18 year old, I very much welcomed the absolute freedom away from my parents and was eagerly looking forward to the challenges ahead of me. With my mind full of such feelings and my stomach full of fish and chips, I drifted into a deep sleep with an optimistic smile on my face.

A sample of my favourite Iranian appetizers/ side dishes.

Sabzee- Fresh herb salad (basil, tarragon, mint etc.) with radishes and spring onions. Even more delicious with feta cheese and walnuts.

Mirza Ghasemi- A tasty dish (from Gilan province, by the Caspian Sea) of soft roasted aubergine in tomato and garlic sauce with eggs cooked into it. I garnish this dish with fried egg and nigella seeds or crushed peppercorns.

Salad-eh-Shirazi- This salad consists of a seasoned mixture of finely diced cucumber, aromatic tomatoes, onion, fresh finely chopped mint, lime juice, balsamic vinegar and virgin olive oil.

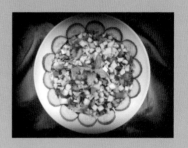

Must-o-Mooseer (Far left of the photo) - Seasoned plain yoghurt with finely chopped Iranian wild garlic (*Mooseer*). Using wild shallots will also do

Torshi-eh-Liteh- Pickled mixture of finely diced aubergines, carrots, cauliflower, garlic with a few other vegetables and herbs.

*Must-o-Kheeyar (*Similar to Indian raita) - Seasoned yoghurt with grated cucumber & finely chopped dill/mint).

Salad-eh Olivieh (See Chap. 5)

7

Chelow with Tahdig

(*Persian* style, fluffy rice with rice or potato crackling)   For 6 people

600 g of long grain Basmati rice (I use a brand called Tilda which I believe to be one of the best)

3 tbsps. salt for soaking and 2 tsp. for parboiling the rice

100ml pure vegetable oil & a knob of butter

A pinch of high quality Iranian Saffron strands

2 medium size potatoes (optional)

1. Wash the rice thoroughly in a few changes of cold water to get rid of the excess starch. Cover the rice with cold water and stir in 3 tbsp. salt (you will wash this out later) and soak for at least two hours.

2. About an hour or so before eating, drain the rice and then rinse with warm water, stirring gently with a fork to separate the grains. Half fill a large non-stick saucepan with water and bring to a rapid boil. Stir in the rice and 2 tsp. salt.

3. Boil vigorously for three minutes or so until the rice is parboiled. Stir lightly with a fork during boiling and if necessary add more boiling water to prevent the rice grains from sticking to each other.

4. When the rice grains appear whiter, have nearly doubled in size and break when squeezed firmly between finger and thumb (not as complicated as it sounds!), drain in a colander and lightly rinse under cold water to wash out the remaining starch and excess salt.

5. Wash the pan, return it to the stove and add the vegetable oil, knob of butter and two tablespoons of water and heat rapidly till sizzling. Cover the base of the pan with a layer of potato slices (about 0.8 cm thick) or scatter a thin layer of parboiled rice over the sizzling oil. This layer, which forms a delicious golden crispy base, is called *Tahdig*. Having Persian rice without *Tahdig* is like having roast pork without the crackling.

6. Still on a high heat, scatter over the rest of the parboiled rice, into a pyramid shape.

7. To assist steaming leave at least a clear space of about 1 cm or so below the rim of the saucepan and using a fork make a couple of deep holes in the rice. Wrap the pan lid in a moistened tea towel to form a tight seal when the lid is on. Reduce the heat after 3 minutes or so and steam the rice on a low heat for about 45 minutes.

You'll know when the rice is ready by gently tapping a wet finger on the side of the pan you'll hear a sizzling sound!

8. Towards the end of cooking, grind the saffron strands in a pestle and mortar (a small cube of sugar helps with grinding). Mix it in a small bowl with 3 tbsp. of hot but not boiling water. Let it brew for a few minutes (Liquid Saffron) and then gently stir in a few desert spoons of the cooked white rice.

9. To serve, plunge the bottom of the pan into a couple of inches of cold water in the sink. Then cover the pan with an inverted serving platter and carefully turn the saucepan upside down to transfer the rice and its *Tahdig crown* onto the platter. Garnish the edge of the platter with saffron rice. Or alternatively without turning the saucepan, carefully serve the rice on individual plates with a garnish of saffron rice and a portion of crispy, delicious *Tahdig*. Pouring melted butter over saffron rice gives it a lovely sheen.

10. Enjoy with Kebabs (Chpt. 9) or with a variety of Persian stews (*Khoresht* – Chpts. 3/4/6/11/12).

Crispy Potato *Tahdig*

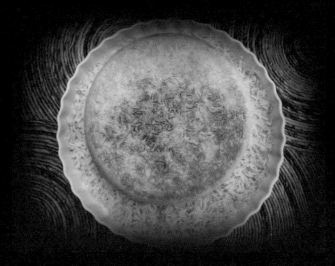

Fluffy saffron rice

Sabzee polo Mahee

(Herb rice with fried fish)

For 6 people

500g of long grain Basmati rice

3 tbsps. salt for soaking & 3 tsp. for parboiling the rice)

250ml pure vegetable oil & 2 knobs of butter

A pinch of high quality Iranian saffron strands

6 large filleted pieces of Sea Bass, Haddock, Cod, smoked Caspian Kutum or Salmon.

Fresh parsley, coriander, dill, chives or spring onion. A small bunch of each. Finely chopped

Less preferably you could use 4 good handfuls of dried Sabzee polo (sold in most Turkish food shops) but you'd need to soak and then drain off the liquid.

Wedges of lemon or lime or Seville oranges if you can get them (In Iran we traditionally use Seville oranges '*Narenj*')

Salt & pepper

1 tsp. turmeric (if unsmoked haddock or cod is used)

4 cloves of garlic, finely chopped

1. Wash, trim and chop the herbs roughly.

2. Sweat the chopped garlic in 100ml of oil, add the herbs, a knob of butter and fry till the mixture is cooked. About 10 minutes on a medium heat would do.

3. Follow steps 1-5 for *Chelow* with *Tahdig*.

4. Set aside a few desert spoons of plain parboiled rice for making a saffron rice garnish. Scatter the rest of the rice over the *Tahdig* in thin layers, alternating layers of rice with layers of herbs. Mix lightly with a fork, shaping it into a pyramid. Place the plain rice by the side on top.

5. Follow steps 7-9 for *Chelow* with *Tahdig*.

6. A few minutes before serving simply fry pieces of fish in a little oil (skin side first). Add seasoning and serve with wedges of lemon, lime or preferably *Narenj* alongside your aromatic *Sabzee Polo,* topped with your favourite crispy *Tahdig*.

Hint: Although I prefer using Sea bass or salmon, *Sabzee polo* is also delicious with smoked haddock or cod. For using unsmoked ones, first dust them lightly in seasoned flour with a teaspoon of turmeric before frying.

This dish is particularly delicious with the Caspian Kutum but you may find only smoked ones elsewhere apart from Iran and adjacent places by the Caspian Sea.

Sabzee polo Mahee

(Herbed rice with fried white fish)

Chips or Sabzee polo?

CHAPTER 2

The Blue Cadillac & Tiffin Boxes

When my mother was alive, I took an old photograph album to her bed-sit which was in an annex of our house. The album was full of family and friends' black and white photographs from the 1950's and 60's. Most of these were taken by my father and many were of my beautiful, elegant, sophisticated and fashion-conscious mum.

In common with many other middle and upper-class Persian housewives in the 50s, Mum was very familiar with the latest western trends and fashions and used to dress like the Hollywood stars she saw in magazines. Mum had a stunning face with bold brows, black hair, high sculpted cheekbones and she loved to wear vivid red lipstick. Her photo would not be out of place next to photos of Ingrid Bergman and Katharine Hepburn. Friends tell me that most Iranian women still are very fashion conscious, but since the Islamic revolution of 1979 and the end of the monarchy, they have either willingly or unfortunately by force, had to conceal their fine clothing under a veil (*chador*) and a long tunic or coat (manteau), which covers everything except their face, hands and feet.

One photo in the album shows that I must have flown with Iran Air before August 1974. It appears that my first flying experience was in a Viscount 700 which carried only about 65 passengers. As I was only two years old at the time, I obviously have no recollection of it. I know, however, that we were travelling from Rezaieh (now known as Urumieh) back to Tehran. The City of Rezaieh is named after Reza Shah-eh Kabir (Reza Shah the Great) the founder of the Pahlavi Dynasty (1925-1979). This city is located within the Azerbaijan region in the north west of Iran, by the western shore of the largest lake in the country. Lake Urumieh is a salt lake that is believed to have therapeutic benefits, especially for rheumatism.

In 1954 my father, who was a Major (*Jenab Sarghord*) in the Royal Army, was commissioned to Rezaieh for a few years. He didn't want to be away from his family for any length of time, so decided to take my mother and my two elder brothers with him. My mother was heavily pregnant with me at the time. It's said that unborn babies can hear their parents and are aware of other sounds. I wonder now if I heard the 'choo choos' of the gigantic steam train in the background, as we travelled from Tehran's only train station to Rezaieh. The sound always has a womb-like comforting quality about it for me, even today.

I have only dim memories of the town of Rezaieh where I was born. I remember the shadows of a tall mulberry tree and an old wooden ladder propped up against the front wall of an old, single storey, mud clad outbuilding, with a few well weathered timber framed windows. I remember being on the roof of this building, picking and gorging on large, juicy, white Persian mulberries. I don't remember how I got onto the rooftop, as I was a bit young to have climbed the ladder myself!

One photograph that was taken in Rezaieh shows my maternal grandmother, who Mum always said adored me because I smiled all the time.

My parents told me many fascinating things about the towns and villages to the west of the Caspian Sea, and about the history of the area. I do hope that one day my family and I will be able to visit Iran, even if only as tourists, to witness its wonderful history and fabulous landscapes.

I can see myself visiting the many mausoleums and memorials such as those of Hafez, Saadi and Omar Khayyam, and imagine soothing all my middle-aged aches and pains by lying in the therapeutic lake at Rezaieh. I often imagine visiting the many historical sites, fascinating artesian wells and caves, wandering through the lush green and fruitful walled gardens. Who knows, maybe sometime in the future, I may be lucky enough to be able to share the exploration of my homeland with my dear readers.

Lying along the old silk route, Iran's, once-great empire was a source of wisdom, tolerance and knowledge, and like Greece and Italy, still has the remains of many ancient palaces and temples, many over 2500 years old.

It's interesting that in 539 B.C the Persian king Cyrus the Great, having conquered the city of Babylon, freed all the slaves, declared that all people had the right to choose their own religion, and established racial equality. These and other decrees were recorded on Cyrus's (baked-clay) Cylinder which has been recognised as the world's first charter of human rights. Although I'm very proud to be a British Iranian, I'm now ashamed of and worried by the current political and religious unrest in Iran and the lack of freedom in my beloved homeland. How my once civilised and peaceful country has fallen under today's regime baffles me, and so many of my fellow exiles.

When my dad's commission in Rezaieh ended, *Jenab Sarghord* Payami's family, now with an extra member, (me of course) returned to the capital, Tehran. I have no clear recollection of my first three years or so in Tehran. My earliest memory is of being picked up every school-day in a huge light blue and white American made car, most probably a Cadillac. I was always the last pupil to be picked up and myself and another boy were often able to sit comfortably in the front seat next to the driver. I don't know about the law these days in Iran, but there was no law then about the number of passengers allowed in a car, there could sometimes be six of us plus the driver!

In the boot of the Cadillac there would be six battered school bags and six, three or four-tiered, stainless steel tiffin lunch boxes. I usually had a four-tiered version. The bottom compartment would contain various seasonal fruits such as pomegranates, Sharon fruits, mouth-watering apricots, both red and black cherries and in the box above it a king sized custard donut *(Pirushkee)*. The upper two boxes contained plain steamed rice (*Chelow*) and a stew *(khoresht)*. Sometimes my tiffin was a three-tiered version because the top compartment contained a mixed rice and meat dish (*polo*). One of these polo dishes, which some of our friends in London love so much, is called *Lubia Polo*.

The upper two boxes were always given to the dinner lady to be warmed up for lunch. Every day she would carry this out with dozens of tiffin boxes for her hungry charges.

After I had completed my elementary education at this lovely primary school, I went on to a nearby public school called Amir Ataback. I hated it. The school had a small playground to the rear of the main building which was surrounded on three sides by dwarf brick parapet walls, surmounted by a metal fence. "L" shaped, rusty metal hooks were welded to the posts so we could hang up our school bags and coats during play time. The playground was often where the headmaster or his deputy meted out punishment and humiliation to those boys that were deemed (not always rightly) to have been misbehaving. For this purpose, a wooden bench and a cane were always placed there.

One day whilst playing football, I accidently hit a boy on the back of his head with the ball. Had he not been standing on the boundary parapet wall he would have been okay and would have escaped any injuries, but he was facing the street and right in front of his forehead was the dreaded rusty hook. Blood poured down the poor boy's face. I asked someone to call the headmaster, ran towards the unlucky boy, apologised and tried to comfort him. When I examined the wound I realised that both the boy and I had been lucky. Had the hook been fixed a few inches lower or had he been a taller boy then the impact would have caused serious injury to his eyes. The boy was taken off to a local clinic where he received several stitches.

A few hours after this incident, the playground bell rang three times and I, for the first and last time, was asked to lie on the dreaded wooden bench, face down with one bare foot up. I must have received at least twice the number of painful lashes on my feet than the boy had stitches to his forehead.

The following day, my dad was summoned to the school, and upon his arrival in full army uniform, was informed of my apparent stupidity and carelessness in the playground. According to the Head, I should have noticed the boy standing on the parapet wall and should have kicked the ball more gently. I was then told off again at home, this time on the grounds that the injury could have been more serious, resulting in the boy dying and myself being charged with manslaughter. The whole scenario seems ridiculous to me now, because if the same incident were to happen in any school in Britain today, it's likely that the school would be in trouble for ignoring its health and safety obligation, rather than the child for his carelessness.

Surprisingly, no attempt was made by the school to prevent the recurrence of such an incident and the dreaded hooks remained, an eyesore for me and (literally perhaps) for some other unfortunate boys for many years.

The humiliation meted out to me in this school didn't stop there, and a few months later I unfortunately experienced it again. This time I was punished for not doing my homework. I knew exactly what happened to boys who didn't hand in their homework on time, and so could have avoided the punishment. I was asked to take my school bag to the corner of the classroom, to hold it on my head facing towards my class mates, to raise and bend one foot and to stay motionless for an hour. As a result I missed the entire lesson and the homework that was set for it, and thus found myself in a vicious circle! The valuable lesson I learnt was to simply do my homework or, if for whatever reason I failed to do so, to at least make sure that my bag was absolutely empty on that day! This type of punishment was effective in Iran back in 1960s, and somehow seemed to work much better than the rather less arduous after-school detentions that are handed out in UK schools today.

During the same early period of my life, I met my first best friend. His name was Kamran, which is pronounced 'come-run' in Persian. Kamran used to live in my neighbourhood and his house was so close to ours that we could talk to each other from our flat roof tops.

In those days not many people in Iran had colour televisions, but both of our families did and we also had the largest screens available as well. Every weekend Kamran and I used to take turns to ask all our friends over to our houses to watch the TV together. We used to create a 'cinema' by placing 10 or more folding chairs in rows in our TV room and in order to enhance the experience even served pistachio nuts, salted and roasted almonds or sunflower and melon seeds and ice lollies during the advertisements.

We also used to frequently play on our flat roof tops, oblivious to any danger. Many enjoyable hours were spent playing Cowboys and Indians and sharing ghost stories.

Kamran and I were close companions for years and kept in touch even when we were no longer neighbours, but eventually 'out of sight out of mind' as the saying goes, applied to us and we communicated less frequently. However, I honoured our good friendship some 30 years or so later by naming my son Cameron.

Mum & Dad's wedding – 1941

Unti Monireh & unkle Sheyda   *Unkle Sheyda & Dad on the righ*

Grandpa Allahverdi & grandma Vasangheezi (maternal side) - Rezaieh Sea

Mum in the 80's (why?)

My elegant mum in the 50's

Mum, Dad, my two brothers & I (a twinkle in my dad's green eyes)

In the front- Grandma & grandad (Paternal side)

At the back- Unti Monireh, uncles & Dad (second right)-70's

Train journey to Rezaieh - Mum, Dad, my two brothers and I in the tummy

Flight journey back from Rezaieh - I'm on the far right

Left to right- Dad, unti Monireh, uncle Bijan & grandma Tooba (30's)

Mum, Dad, grandparents (maternal side) & me

According to Mum, I never had tantrums and was a sweet little boy.

Lovely shoes!

(I think Mum wanted her third child to be a girl.)

There was a very good reason for Mum dressing me like this! (Circumcision)

Left to right- Unti Monireh & Dad
at the back, great grandma &
grandma Tooba in the front

Left to right- Grandad Allahverdi,
unckle Sheyda, grandad Habib at the
back, grandma Vasangheeze , unti
Monireh & Mum in the front

Lubia polo

(Cumin scented rice with French beans & minced meat)   For 6 people

450 g long grain Basmati rice

3 tbsp. salt for soaking and 2 tsp. for parboiling the rice

200ml pure vegetable oil & 2 knobs of butter

A pinch of high quality Iranian saffron strands

400g of fresh or frozen French beans

400g minced beef or lamb

1 large onion, chopped

2 tbsp. cinnamon

2 tsp. cumin powder

1tsp turmeric

1 tbsp. cumin seeds

120g tomato paste

1 tin of chopped tomatoes

Salt & pepper

1. Chop the French beans into 1cm pieces or alternatively use frozen chopped beans. Bring a pan of slightly salted water to the boil and parboil the beans for about 3 minutes. Drain & set aside.

2. In a large and deep non-stick pan, fry the chopped onion in 100ml of vegetable oil for a few minutes until golden. In the same pan seal the mince and then stir in the cumin powder, turmeric and cinnamon. Stir in the tomato paste and tinned tomatoes. Add enough hot water to cover the mixture. Give it a stir, bring to the boil, and then reduce to a simmer for 10 minutes. Don't let it dry out-you want it saucy. Add a knob of butter, stir in the parboiled beans and season to taste.

3. In the meantime prepare plain rice, following steps 1-5 for *Chelow* with *Tahdig* (Chpt.1), using much bigger saucepan.

4. Set aside a few dessertspoons of plain parboiled rice (for making the saffron garnish). Scatter a thin layer of rice over the *Tahdig*, sprinkle two pinches of cumin seeds on top and add a layer of the mince and French bean mixture. Mix the two layers lightly with fork and continue the same layering process, shaping the mixed rice into a pyramid. Place the plain rice by the side on top.

5. Follow steps 7-9 for *Chelow* with *Tahdig* (Chpt.1).

Hint: To make this dish extra special, you could add 100-200g of cooked diced shin of beef into your mixture (Step 2).

Lubia polo

(Cumin scented rice with French beans & diced/minced mea

Kamran, You may be out of sight, but

you're never out of mind.

My first best friend Kamran

CHAPTER 3

Kippers & Sheep's Head

My first night in London was over, the noise of traffic waking me up. I went down to the hotel's cosy breakfast room and was warmly welcomed by a lady there. I remember that she had a very strong, probably Irish, accent and although choosing the right hot refreshment was no problem, I struggled to order the breakfast. She asked me kippers or English? After uttering a string of hopeful 'yes pleases' and 'maybes' she understood that my English was not very good, but I made her smile and got both kippers and a full English breakfast, at no extra charge!

What a lovely breakfast it was, and although I was not used to this type of food, I welcomed it and returned my plate licked clean. In Iran, breakfast usually consists of a small portion of feta cheese (*Paneer*) or butter & jam (*Kareh-o-morab ba*), sweetened black tea (*Chi* or *Chaee*) in a special tea glass and warm Persian bread, from a local bakery (*Nanvaee*). The bread arrives freshly baked and still hot, courtesy of the baker's delivery man. Having said that, other things such as butterscotch with honey (*Sar-Sheer-o-Assal*), sugar melon with ham (*Kharboozeh ba jambon*) and porridge (*Halim*) are also sometimes served. And on occasions a freshly cooked delicate and tasty dish of sheep's head and hooves called *Kaleh Patcheh* is also eaten for breakfast, especially in winter time.

Talking about the tasty parts of a sheep's head reminds me of one of my best friends in London, Ali A. One morning Ali wanted to impress and surprise his new English girlfriend, so he rose very early without waking her, and prepared this special Persian breakfast dish. When the poor girl woke up, Ali asked her to lift the lid on a large saucepan, which was still on a burner, to admire what he had cooked. The poor girl was shocked to see a pair of sheep's eyes staring back at her from within the saucepan, first thing in the morning too! However, I believe that she did ask Ali to cook her the same dish many times after that.

Anyway, back to the main story. After breakfast, I carefully unstitched my back pocket and visited the nearest bank. Having handed over my £100 and uttering many yeses and maybes, I managed to make myself understood. I opened a deposit account in which the fees for my A' level education and money for my accommodation could be deposited by my parents direct from Iran. The money they sent was adequate, but not enough for me to enjoy the same standard of living as most of my friends. My parents would not have hesitated to send me more, but I knew they were struggling financially, especially with three sons abroad, so I avoided asking and decided that I should find a part time job very soon.

The accommodation officer's suggestion proved to be a good one, and a week's temporary stay somewhere else was all worthwhile. I couldn't possibly have found better accommodation than at Hanna's home. Hanna, her immediate family and friends were very kindly, caring, understanding and warm. Her house soon became my second home and fortunately (or sometimes unfortunately) she acted like a mum to me when my own mum was over 3300 miles away.

Initially I believed that all girls in the UK were very fond of Middle Eastern men like me. We were supposedly the tall (not in my case sadly) dark and handsome (again possibly not in my case!) romantic suitors of their dreams! I knew for a fact that some even travelled to foreign resorts for sun, sea and sex with tall, dark and handsome locals. What I didn't yet know, was that the temptation to sleep with an overseas student with very little English was not as strong as the temptation to indulge in the same activities with a handsome waiter whilst on holiday!

Before coming to London, I was told that people in England were very polite. So polite that they even used the word 'please' to ask someone to shut up! Bearing this in mind I confidently expected that if I very politely asked an attractive girl for a slow dance, I wouldn't be refused. I was wrong, very wrong indeed, and some painful experiences resulted!

One night I visited a popular local nightclub which boasted live music. The stage had a rotating floor and so when one of the bands wanted to have a break the stage would rotate 180 degrees and the second band would start playing. They were playing the best of the 1960's and the latest 1970's soul & funk music. Most of the teenagers and foreign students like myself were inexperienced, would look hopefully for someone attractive, and then nervously wait until nearly closing time till the final slow songs played, before asking for a dance. Some were more successful than others.

"May I have a dance with you?" a handsome Persian friend of mine politely asked a very attractive girl, sitting at a nearby table with two other girls.

"Oh f**k off you", the girl said. My friend was shocked but he, like many other hopefuls, was not going to give up trying to get a dance with an English girl.

He then bent over his no. 2 target who was sitting at the same table.

Would you like a dance with me? He begged. "No thank you" the girl replied, feeling sorry for him.

"What about you then?" he asked the third, and rather an unattractive girl.

"No p**s off you w*****" the girl said, with a winning grin on her face.

Although I cannot see any justification for those and other girls' rudeness to a bunch of desperate foreign students with moustaches, I have to be frank here, when I look back I can understand the girls' frustration at being endlessly approached and hassled by a long stream of testosterone driven, hot blooded foreigners with funny accents.

Personally I was choosy. I was looking for an 'inner beauty' but with an outward appearance that I would also find attractive! To this end I was not after an 'easy' girl and so, after spotting and monitoring my target, I would deliberately wait for her to reject a few applicants! This would reassure me that my target met my exacting standards! I would then, with all the pride and arrogance of Mr Darcy in 'Pride & Prejudice', back straight and head up, approach my target, secretly crossing my fingers that I would succeed.

I monitored the situation closely at my chosen girl's table for quite some time and my observation was duly noticed by the girls. I decided that my friend's target no. 2 would be a suitable person for me to request a dance with.

"May I have the pleasure of having a dance with you?" I, very politely but somewhat awkwardly asked her.

"No thank you," the girl replied

"Why not? Music no good for dancing?"

"You are not f***ing good. Why don't you and your friends get it, we are not interested. Ok. You prat?" The other two girls giggled.

I was humiliated and speechless, so left with my tail well and truly between my legs. I felt very sorry for myself and my friends and genuinely couldn't understand our lack of success. It seemed we could carry on asking girls to dance and be rejected for the rest of that night.

After a restless night, I concluded that the rejections were possibly due to my having a beard. It certainly never crossed my mind that it could have been my approach that was wrong, and that I was too polite. Although George Best had a beard and was certainly successful with the ladies, I became convinced that mine had to go. I did however keep the moustache for a while.

Many Iranian students back in the 1970's looked, behaved, walked and even talked like Borat of later TV fame. Even after shaving off my beard, I still suffered one rejection after another, accompanied by various expletives; this made me think that perhaps it was due to my moustache. So that went too.

My landlady, Hanna, turned out to be a cross between a mother and a sister to me and gave lots of valuable advice on the dating front! I quickly learnt that asking a girl for a dance in a club, didn't require making a speech and simply the question "dance?" with a genuine smile would suffice. Better still, of course, would be to have a chat with the target at the bar beforehand. I was finally learning.

Sometimes Hanna felt free to give her opinion about my dates. I recall her telling me "Mehrdad, surely you cannot go out with a girl called Gertrude" My apologies here to anyone called Gertrude.

She also advised that if the chemistry was right, on the second date, I should not let them go home without a kiss, or better still ask her back to my place. Failing to do either of the above, 8 out of 10 girls would think that I was either boring, a virgin, insufficiently experienced, or possibly differently inclined. Hanna's assessment was right and I began to be a little more successful!

On a more serious note Hanna was instrumental in helping me to gain confidence and be accepted among other young British students.

Hanna had many students stay in her house previously, but apparently none of them had been granted the privileges she allowed me to have in her home. She seemed very happy with my tidiness, personality, manners, personal hygiene and above all my positive influence on her 10 year old son, David. Consequently, after a few weeks she told me that I should feel at home there, because I respected her home like my own.

She would often take me sight-seeing, swimming, to her friends' parties etc. and occasionally she would even let me borrow her size 9 ice-skating boots. That was another skill learned.

In summer when I had to return home to see my family, Hanna & David would take me all the way to Heathrow airport. On my return, after twelve hours flying, queuing, being questioned by passport control, queuing some more, unpacking and repacking my suitcase for Customs, it was lovely to see them both welcoming me back home again to London.

In the early hours of one morning, after a night of clubbing, I noticed a small fruit bowl on the dining room table. In Iran typically fruit bowls are huge and laden with fruit in case of unexpected guests! In this bowl there was only a bunch of grapes, a few cherries, one banana and two peaches. I'm afraid I ate the lot. Later that morning I noticed that Hanna was a bit subdued, so I asked her if she was ok. She told me "Mehrdad do you recall me telling you that you should feel at home here?" I replied that I did, "Well I didn't mean that you should feel at home to an extent that you completely empty the fruit bowl. David wanted some fruit this morning and the bowl was empty." I was ashamed of myself, so in the afternoon I returned home, before Hanna arrived, with two carrier bags full of fruit. I filled up the fruit bowl and left the rest in the fridge. When Hanna came home she simply smiled and good humour was restored.

A few days after this I decided to surprise them one evening by cooking a Persian dish. Unfortunately though I added too much fenugreek and it made the dish a bit bitter. I decided to share the dish with my friends instead.

I wasn't trying to impress my friends and they weren't expecting a lot from me, because I had never cooked a Persian or any other dish before that day. The dish was a herb stew called *Khoresht-eh Ghormeh Sabzee*, which is served with fluffy steamed rice (*Chelow*- Chpt.1). My friends missed Persian food so much that they didn't even notice the bitterness and gratefully handed me back clean plates.

The majority of my Iranian friends in the college had no intention of working. However as previously mentioned, I didn't want to place additional financial pressure on Mum and Dad, but I did want to wear fashionable clothes, go to nice clubs and restaurants and not penny pinch, so I knew I had to find myself a reasonable part time job, sooner rather than later.

With some difficulty I managed to obtain a student work permit and shortly thereafter got my first job. I chose to apply to a local night club for several reasons. Firstly it was a weekend job and wouldn't interfere too much with my studies, also the job didn't require a full command of English! The pay was enough to cover my rent and food at Hanna's, and of course it would give me the opportunity to meet more girls!

My new work-mate and mentor was Barbara. Barbara had ginger curly hair, was funny and warm. She taught me everything I needed to know about the work within an hour. Apart from flirting with Barbara, my duties consisted of frying hamburgers or preparing chicken with chips, placing them in a basket with a few leaves of lettuce and serving filtered coffee. Chicken in a basket, those were the days!

The only downside was that the club required me to wear a ridiculous yellow shirt and a black velvet bowtie. Unfortunately the yellow shirt bore much evidence of its previous owner in the form of sweat stains and a singularly unpleasant odour.

Barbara and I made a good team and within a few nights the turnover of our section of the club more than doubled. I didn't chat Barbara up though, as I felt I needed to preserve a good working relationship! However, this didn't stop us flirting and certainly made our shifts pass more quickly.

I was very much enjoying my first ever job, but when I decided to buy my own yellow shirt and black velvet bow tie, things changed. The manager in charge of us one night noticed that I wasn't wearing the uniform that I had been asked to wear, and questioned me about it. I told him that the shirt was soiled and smelly. This didn't satisfy him and he asked why I was wearing a new bowtie, to which I answered that it made me appear smarter. I asked him why he wasn't happy with this answer to which he replied "If you look smart like this then what is the difference between you and me?"

Well I said "the only difference is that I work this side of the bar and you work on the other side". How to make friends and influence people!

I didn't want to lose my job over such a trivial matter so I tried to compromise. The morning after, I disinfected the shirt that he wanted me to wear, hand washed it several times and rinsed it in a solution of …. wait for it… Brut aftershave. The next time I worked, I wore the required shirt with my own bowtie. However, this particular manager was not working every weekend and so I used to wear the new shirt when he was not on duty.

One particular night, the person who cleaned the main kitchen didn't turn up and all the greasy appliances and equally greasy floor needed to be cleaned. This was my manager's opportunity to even up the score. After Barbara and I cleaned up our section and were just about to go home (about 2am) this manager asked me to go to the main kitchen to clean up. No mention of this kind of work had been made at my interview or since, so I told him surely he could ask other kitchen staff to stay behind and do it. As you can imagine this didn't go down well either. When I look back I'm not sure if I was just being bolshie or really quite justified.

After Barbara had gone, he told me that I had no choice except to do as he asked. The kitchen had to be properly cleaned for the next day and I was the man to do it. As annoyed as I was, I realised that since they owed me wages, if I refused I would probably never see the money they owed. I also realised that I enjoyed working with Barbara and that the money they were paying me was quite good. I soon found myself skidding about on my trendy platform shoes. It was a miserable job and on my way home as dawn was breaking, I decided to quit.

Barbara did try to change my mind, but the decision was made.

A few days later, Barbara called to tell me that the arrogant manager was going to be off duty that weekend, so I went to visit her. I arrived at the club quite late and found Barbara very busy and single handed. We didn't have the chance to talk, but she did pass me a basket of fried chicken and chips. I so wanted to jump over the counter, give her a hug and help her, but since I was no longer an employee I didn't.

After I left I still didn't ask Barbara for a date. Somehow a rejection from her would have been more painful than a rejection from someone I didn't know.

I visited Barbara a few times after that, but soon discovered some more classy clubs in central London, and I didn't see her then for a couple of years.

I had managed to save quite a bit of money and soon bought my first car. It was a good second hand car and thanks to Hanna's advice and negotiating skills I got a reasonable discount from the dealer for paying in cash.

Hanna's husband Donny, whom I respected very much, owned a pub and also a cosy Latin American night club, which was located in a cellar in the west end of London. One day he asked if I would be interested in earning a few quid on a regular basis, a few nights of the week, giving lifts to his nightclub customers. He told me that local mini-cab firms were unreliable and that his customers would welcome someone like me, who was friendly and trustworthy, to provide a sort of personal transport service between their homes and the club.

Donny also told me that whilst I worked there I would be free to socialise with his clients and would get my food and drink free of charge. I accepted his offer without hesitation. Hanna wisely advised me to be wary, as people could turn nasty with a drink inside them. I don't think this had entered into my considerations.

Working and especially socialising in Donny's night club was great fun and I loved the general atmosphere, the food and the music. On my first visit Donny introduced me to some of his regular clients and I soon managed to find other clients as well. Some of them even asked me to pick them up from their homes and agreed the return time.

I quickly realised that most of the clients left the club just after closing time and therefore by the time I had made one or two short journeys, they would all have gone home and I would have no more customers. This clearly wasn't going to work out, so somehow I had to sort this problem.

I shared my concerns with a few of my clients and offered them a free, pick up service if they would agree to leave the club at various times in the hour before closing time. A reasonable number of them agreed with my plan and from then on they would leave the club whenever I was free to drive them home. They were very generous with their tips so soon my earnings had increased significantly.

I guess that this was the first work problem that I had come up with a creative solution for. It was a skill that would stand me in good stead.

Although things were much more relaxed back in the 70's and many people used to earn good money for doing unofficial mini cabbing, I was not licensed or insured to carry any passengers for a business. I knew all my passengers personally so as far as I was concerned, at that time, it was like giving a lift to a few friends. However, I must admit that they used to give me more money than the going mini cab rates, and realise now that I could have been in big trouble with the Police.

On one occasion I really did something rash; after finishing my normal work I agreed to give a lift to a complete stranger who happened to be drunk. Surprisingly when he sat in my car he handed over a £20 note. He was so drunk that any kind of conversation beyond finding out his destination was impossible. After a few miles when I had stopped at some traffic lights, he suddenly opened the door, got out of the car, banged the door shut and without a word ran away. I pondered a bit and then came to the conclusion that the man must have forgotten about the £20 and was doing a runner. This does still bring a smile to my face!

Donny was very calm, very good to his customers and would make sure that they all had a good night. A few unfamiliar rather rough looking guys came to the night club one evening. Donny was not sure about their presence in his club, but I guess in the end thought their money would be the same as that of his regulars. These guys had a very good night, a good dinner and ordered a lot of drinks but when it came to the payment they refused.

Donny very politely approached them and asked if there was anything wrong with their meal. They shook their heads from side to side and just giggled like children. Donny, still with a smile on his face, asked them if they'd had a good night, to which they replied "Without a doubt". At this point the smile suddenly left Donny's face and he whispered something like "the night is not over yet". He told them once more that immediate payment was expected. They shook their heads again. Not wanting to disturb the rest of the patrons, Donny left the four guys alone. They made their way up the stairs and out into the street. None of the staff I knew followed these guys up the stairs. I asked Donny if he was going to let them leave like this without paying, but he was so uptight that he didn't even answer.

After a while, I went upstairs to take one of the regulars home. There was a big fight a few meters away from the club. The four guys, who had refused to pay earlier, were outnumbered by at least six heavily muscled men. In a matter of seconds all four lay on the pavement soaked in their own blood. Their wallets and their other valuables taken from them. The muscle men then vanished into thin air just before the police vans arrived at the scene. At this point Donny came up and made a formal complaint about the men refusing to pay for the services they'd received earlier. How the muscle guys managed to materialised within a few minutes and if they had anything to do with the event in the club, I never managed to find out. However I came to the conclusion that nice as he was, Donny was not a man to be messed with. I wouldn't have been surprised to hear that each one of them had woken up the next morning with a dead horse in the bed next to them!

I stayed with Hanna for 2 years, and although I very much enjoyed being in her home, one thing was missing. That was the freedom to come and go anytime I pleased, and to have people stay overnight whenever I wished. So although Hanna and her family tried to keep me there, I felt it was time to move on.

I managed to find a basic but cosy bed-sit in a large house, a mile or so from Hanna's. Again I was very lucky, Chani the landlord, proved to be as caring and a kindly decent person, just as Hanna.

1976 – Working with curly Barbara

(My first job in the U.K.)

Early 80's – With Muffin

What a poser

Khoresht-eh Ghormeh Sabzee

(Lamb/beef casserole with herbs & kidney beans)   For 6 people

600g diced shoulder of lamb or shin of beef

Fresh coriander, parsley, spinach & chives - 1 bunch of each (discarding the woody stalks)

1 tbsp. dried fenugreek

1 large onion - finely chopped

6 dried Persian Limes (soaked and pricked)

2 tbsp. sour grape juice or juice of a lime

2 tins red kidney beans

1 tsp. turmeric

2 tsp. cinnamon powder

1 tsp. tomato paste

Salt and pepper for seasoning

4 tbsp. olive or any other pure vegetable oil

2 knobs of butter

1. Trim & discard any fat around the meat and cut into small 2cm cubes.

2. Clean, wash and finely chop the fresh herbs. Alternatively you can use a handful each of the dried version of the same herbs or 4 handfuls of ready packed *Sabzee Ghormeh* which can be purchased from all Iranian and many Turkish stores. (Dried herbs work better if soaked briefly in little warm water).

3. Fry the chopped onion in 1 tbsp. vegetable oil until golden brown and set aside. In the same pan sauté the fresh or soaked dried herbs in 2tbsp. vegetable oil, stirring constantly for about 5 minutes.

4. In a large saucepan, add the remaining oil and seal the meat. When browned and fully sealed add the spices, fried onions, tomato paste and herbs and give the mixture a good stir. Pour over boiling water to form a cover of about 4 cm. Reduce heat and simmer for at least 1 hour 30 minutes. Halfway through cooking add the kidney beans, butter, Persian limes, sour grape juice and seasoning to taste. The casserole needs to be stirred from time to time and if needed, more boiling water should be added to maintain a liquor cover of about 2 cm till the end of cooking.

5. Serve with *Chelow* (Chpt.1) & your favourite side dish/es.

For the Iranian fluffy rice

Ingredients and preparation as per *Chelow* with *Tahdig* (see Chpt.1)

Khoresht-eh Ghormeh Sabzee

(Lamb /beef Casserole with herbs & kidney beans)

A typical daily display of fruits in Persia

CHAPTER 4:

The Donkey Express & the Cross-Eyed People

By the time I was 10, my father had become a top ranking, three star colonel (*Jenab Sarhangeh Setad*). He was in charge of a major barracks to the north of Tehran. The basic salary for officers in the Shah's army was very low indeed, especially compared to other professions, but the perks and privileges were also very good. We had an army servant (*gomashteh*) that we knew as a butler; we got discounted food and supplies from the Army stores; we were also allowed the use of the Army's marquees in nearby woodlands to camp, and each year we spent several weeks at a seaside villa by the Caspian Sea, that was also owned by the Army.

In Iran, two years military service for all able bodied people was compulsory. Iran is a vast country and some conscripts were sent to camps far from home for their training. Some were sent to military hospitals to assist as nurses and orderlies, some were sent to remote villages to improve the welfare and education of the villagers and some were sent to higher ranking officers' homes to act as a servants as part of their service. These servants were allowed to visit their families for only a couple of days every month.

Due to my father's senior rank, we had several *gomashteh* billeted with us, usually for two years at a time. Most were intelligent and well educated; however, we did have a couple that were less well favoured and certainly less honest. Strangely most of our servants were called either Mohamed or Nasser.

On one occasion a certain gomashteh named Nasser was left behind to look after the house, whilst we all went on holiday to the Caspian Sea. We had a large, beautiful and quite valuable silk Persian carpet in our living room, and as a precaution my dad locked the living room door before our departure.

The weather that year was poor and we returned home late one night, a few days earlier than expected. When Nasser saw us, his face paled and he appeared visibly shaken. My dad first asked him if he was ok. He replied "Yes colonel (*baleh Jenab sarhang*)." So what is wrong? Dad asked. "Nothing *Jenab sarhang,* I was just not expecting you back so early" was his reply. Dad read something suspicious on Nasser's face, so he first checked that the living room door was still locked and then checked all the other valuables in the house. Everything seemed to be in order, so concluded that he had just been enjoying having the house to himself and was simply surprised to see us home so soon.

The next morning my mother decided to cook for lunch a meat and eggplant stew (*Khoresht-eh Gheymeh Bademjan*). She went to the storage room to collect some rice to soak and to her horror found that the 40kg bag of rice, which was full when we left, almost empty.

"Nasser, why is the rice container empty?" she asked.

Like a cringing dog with its tail between its legs he replied "Please don't worry about this Mrs Colonel." "(*Narahat nabasheed Khanoomeh Sarhang).*"

"What do you mean don't worry? What happened to our rice stock? " Mother exclaimed.

"Please don't tell the colonel I have used the rice, I will be replacing all that I have used by this afternoon." He stuttered.

"*Seemhut ghatee potee showdeh Nasser?*" Mother shouted, meaning, are your wires tangled up? Or more simply, have you lost your marbles?

When Mum asked him if he'd really used that amount of rice in five days he admitted that he had done so. "No one could consume 8Kg of rice per day" Mother stated. Nasser however seemed unable to provide a rational explanation for the missing rice.

At lunch time Mum saw one of our neighbours, who told her that it was very wise of us to carry out all the decoration works while we were away from home. She then informed Mum that the workmen were very good and they were going in and out of our house every day, very quietly and without making any mess. Since we had not asked for any decoration work to be undertaken, Mum was somewhat puzzled and wondered if our neighbour's wires had also been *ghatee potee showdeh* (tangled).

When dad came home that evening, Mum told him the whole story. He quickly unlocked the living room door, to reveal our beautiful silk Persian carpet covered with a thick layer of mud and lots of footprints!

My father immediately summoned Nasser. Nasser, I recall, was rather tall and heavily muscled in comparison to my father, who was rather short and of a slim build. Dad demanded the full story of what had transpired, and when Nasser began to make frantic excuses, Dad turned and gave him a sharp slap on the cheek. His face reddened and he froze. I had myself, on rare occasions, received a smack on the cheek from my dad and knew what Nasser had just experienced. I think as a child perhaps I had a twinge of sympathy. Looking back, the situation certainly had a bizarre element, as my dad was at least some six inches shorter and half the bulk of Nasser. However he did always have that air of authority

Well, of course Nasser eventually told the truth - that in order to earn some money he had offered to provide all the local workmen with breakfast and lunch whilst we were away and charged them for doing so. To gain access into the living room, he very carefully and skilfully removed the glazing from the garden door every day, reinstating it each evening.

Nasser was asked to leave and was posted to the nearest barracks. His punishment was that he should clean the barrack's toilets and floors for the remainder of his 2 years' service. However after a month or two, Dad decided he had paid his dues and had him transferred to serve in the Kitchens instead!

After the awful Nasser we had the delightful Mohammad from the far away town of Birjand in the south east of the country.

All our military servants after Nasser were notably of small stature. Perhaps my dad's doing?

Not only was Mohammed quite short, but to my great joy was very good at maths. Unbeknown to my parents Mohammed would do all my tricky maths homework! However with their knowledge, he was also able to help prepare me for my maths and other exams.

He was such a decent and charming guy that Dad would often let him visit his family for a much longer period than was usually allowed. He would also let him accompany me and my friends, sometimes for days, when we went exploring in the mountains on the edge of Tehran and the remote unspoilt villages to the north of the capital city. We would, now and again, go for several days on foot, often leaving at night to reach the mountains before sunrise. This part of my teenage life is very precious to me, and I consider this period to be one of the most enjoyable and memorable times of my life.

In summer, to escape the intense heat of the city, a few friends, Mohammed and I, would leave our houses after midnight, and after a few hours walking, joking, talking and generally mucking about, we would reach one of the villages in the mountains outside Tehran. The village of Farahzad to the north west of the capital city, is well over 1500 years old and is particularly famous for its gardens of white mulberries, and its delicious kebabs and tea houses. This was our favourite of all the villages we visited. I don't know what Farahzad looks like today but back in 1973 it was an unspoilt, lush green cool spot with unpolluted fresh air and a flowing crystal clear river running through it. I recall that the river was hugged on both sides for a mile or so by orchards of apricots, pomegranates, all sort of cherries, mature walnut and mulberry trees.

When we approached this village during any season, we could sense its proximity by its rural smell, carried for miles on the welcoming early morning breeze. In the early hours of a spring morning, the vegetation moistened by the dew, gave off an aroma of different blossoms and the outstanding heavenly smell of Salix Acutifolia-Blue Streak (*Bid-Meshk*) used to take our breath away. In memory of my childhood, I now have a south facing garden, which is rich in exotic and Middle Eastern plants that I have cultivated over the past 10 years or more.

In summer, soon after arriving in Farahzad village, we would go to our favourite tea house/garden, and would sit or even lie on wooden beds covered by Persian rugs that sat at the side of the stream. We would sip endless small glasses of refreshing black tea and every fifteen minutes or so, one of the waiters would circle round the tea house with a massive tray, offering us more.

The shimmer of kerosene lights on the stream, before the dawn and the general atmosphere of this place are tattooed forever in my mind. Later in life, returning to Iran even for a short period would be problematic, so for many years I have gone to the Pelion region of mainland Greece, in search of just this innocence and remoteness. This area of Greece is much loved by myself and my family too.

After an hour or so of rest in the tea garden, we would continue our journey up into the mountains. We travelled on foot or on donkeys that we'd hired, using torches to light our way. If we were lucky we could hire large mules, rather than ordinary donkeys. These hardworking animals seemed to have been equipped with some kind of cruise control and automatic pilot. They knew exactly where they were heading and if we wished they would stop at any village on the way to Imamzadeh Dawood, but they were trained not to divert from the route or to stop anywhere else along the way. So if one of us experienced a call of nature between villages it really was hard luck as they just would not stop! They were also programmed to come to a halt when we reached our final destination.

Imamzadeh Dawood is the tomb of one of the grandsons of a famous Shiite Imam. The mausoleum, which has always drawn hordes of pilgrims, is located north west of Tehran, deep in the Alborz Mountains. The donkey track to the holy site from Farahzad was somewhat hazardous. The main reason for this was the traffic that was generated by the Hee-Haw carriages and hordes of pilgrims on foot, all trying to pass each other, in both directions on a narrow and rocky path, all wanting to get to their destinations as quickly as possible.

Many pilgrims carried their sick children, other critically ill members of their family or maybe a lamb or sheep for sacrifice on their backs or on donkeys. On many occasions my legs were badly bruised and trousers ripped from being crushed in between passing Hee-Haws.

On one occasion I was thrown off my mule in the melee. I landed on the sharp edge of a rock and rolled down the slope into the adjacent rocky valley. The worst part was running back up the track, eventually catching up with my mule and somehow getting back on by climbing up above it and landing on the poor animal from a higher level. Several times I would miss the mule altogether and landed on the track. I still have a small scar on my elbow from one such incident. As explained before, the donkeys and mules on this route didn't like stopping anywhere other than at a couple of tea houses and as a consequence were known among us friends as the Donkey Express.

Occasionally we'd follow the Donkey Express route on foot and then we'd break our journey half way, sleeping for a night or two on the pitch black mountain. After finding a suitable spot near a stream, we would set up a tent or two, make a fire, brew tea and cook something very basic to eat and then spend countless hours watching the billions of bright twinkling stars in the night sky.

We were also aware however of the possibility of being attacked by certain highly intelligent beings with upright ears, sharp, pointed muzzles and gleaming yellow eyes. Yes, there were packs of wild wolves in the Alborz Mountains and sometimes, especially in winter, we could hear them howling in the distance.

I recall a neighbour telling us a terrible true story about someone he knew. The poor man was driving along a snow covered remote mountain track not far from Farahzad. In the car, wrapped comfortably in warm blankets, were his wife and two very young children. The car broke down and the man got out trying to repair it and a few minutes later, his poor wife and children watched helplessly as he was set upon by hungry wolves. His wife tried to scare them off by shouting and knocking on the window, but to no avail. To protect her children she had no choice but to wait out the attack in which her husband met a particularly brutal end.

This mountain was also home to other dangerous animals and wildlife including over 60 different varieties of deadly insects, scorpions, snakes, brown bears and even a few rare Persian leopards.

Whilst we did worry a little about such hazards, it certainly didn't quell our teenage sense of adventure.

Scorpions are nocturnal. Nowadays, one can easily identify them in the dark using a Black Light (ultraviolet light) but we didn't have such things back in the seventies. We continuously checked our kit, particularly our trousers and boots, to avoid any painful stings. As a child I was obsessed by scorpions and would collect them by forcing them out of their hiding places by pouring saline water down their burrows and then taking them home to study.

My fascination with these creatures remains, though not my method of capturing them! Scorpions strangely are fluorescent under ultraviolet light. These ancient eight legged creatures are the oldest arthropods and have been in existence for over 430 million years. Based on fossilised remains that have been discovered, they have changed very little in the intervening millennia. Female scorpions are highly cannibalistic and often eat their partners after mating. Thank goodness females of the human species don't do this!

We also knew there were venomous snakes lurking in the undergrowth and in the trees, but at the time that didn't bother us either. I shiver to think of it now! I recall more than once, whilst picking fruit from the white mulberry trees, accidentally grabbing a slumbering snake's head! When looking back I think I was a bit of a youthful Crocodile Dundee.

There were still leopards in the Alborz Mountains, though they were very rare. Many leopard populations worldwide are scattered, fragmented and threatened. These Persian leopards are one of the largest of all the subspecies of leopards in the world. They can stand up to two and a half feet tall at the shoulder, and weigh as much as 155 lbs. We always hoped to see one but never did.

One of the mountain villages not too far along our trek was *Kigah*. We had been warned by other travellers that some of its inhabitants were dangerous and unpredictable. We were also told that apparently many of the villagers, particularly the unpredictable ones, were severely cross-eyed. Legend has it that when the enemies of Imamzadeh Dawood were chasing him through the mountains, trying to kill him, they passed through the village of *Kigah*. When some of the villagers were asked the direction in which he had gone, they daren't say a word but simply showed the way by looking in that direction. Perhaps the wind changed as well, but according to legend the villagers thereafter all bore a terrible squint.

All these possible dangers, the leopards, insects, bears, snakes, scorpions, wolves and cross-eyed people certainly made our trips more thrilling and memorable. However, of all of these exciting hazards I suppose luckily, we only ever came across scorpions and the odd snake.

On our first visit to the holy village of Imamzadeh Dawood, we did see a man with a memorable squint. He was very tall and thin and his piercing light green eyes each pointed away from his long, narrow nose looking off into the distance. We immediately, rightly or wrongly, assumed him to be a *Kigahee* (from Kigah) and later on even blamed him for the theft of my friend's watch. I'm sure the poor guy was innocent of any misdemeanour, but with our imaginations in overdrive, that clearly wasn't what we thought at the time.

All along the mountain track to Imamzadeh Dawood, colourful pieces of cloth and ribbons were tied to the branches of trees and shivered and fluttered in the wind. They were tied by pilgrims hoping that their prayers would be answered much in the way that Tibetan pilgrims do. When I watch TV documentaries today, about the fascinating territories of Tibet and Nepal, it always conjures up memories of my trips in the mountains.

In the village everybody's attention was focused on a troupe of male actors in elaborate costumes in an open theatre, performing a fascinating Persian opera (Ta'zieh). These passion plays or Persian operas are an ancient traditional drama, conveyed mainly through music and singing. Common themes for these plays are heroic tales of love and sacrifice and of resistance against evil.

The Imam Zadeh's tomb was a mix of very old and relatively new construction and was built in a pleasant valley, deep in the mountain. The buildings in the village were made of either old bricks or of Adobe. Adobe is a traditional building material, used mainly in the villages, and is made up from a mix of clay, sand, horse manure and water, bound together with fibre, such as straw. The Adobe material is shaped into bricks and dried hard in the sun. It's an effective and long-lasting building material.

One of our friends who accompanied us on these trips was of a more devout disposition than the rest of us, at least at times when it suited him. We accompanied him into the shrine of Imamzadeh Dawood and at ground level, pilgrims were kissing the smooth and well-worn bars of the metal fencing around the gravestone, praying for their sick relatives and hoping for other miracles.

We soon realised that the actual grave was located below ground level. So we made our way to this part where there were fewer pilgrims, though they were performing the same rituals. We soon discovered that there were several further levels below this level and eventually found our way into a very tiny room that could hold only a few people. We were told that the Imam Zadeh indeed had been buried within this room and that the upper levels had been purely formed to reduce the amount of pilgrims that visited. Access to this tiny room was gained through a small opening within the penultimate level.

Apart from a single candle on the grave, there was no other means of lighting. As we entered the room the candle guttered and died. It was during this absolute darkness that the Kigahee took the opportunity to snatch my friend's watch and simply pass through the opening and walk away, or so we were convinced! One day I will have to return to Persia and visit Kigah and in my mind at least offer my apologies to its residents for our superstitious beliefs and also to see if I can spot any cross-eyed residents!

Whilst we were staying close to the mausoleum, we didn't have to worry about buying any food. Fresh raw meat and vegetables were delivered free to our tent or to the door-step of our rented room. It is customary for each pilgrim to sacrifice a sheep or a lamb, hoping for a miracle cure for their loved ones and this meat was then shared among all the pilgrims and cooked over open fires.

Khoresht-eh Gheymeh Bademjun

(Diced meat stew with aubergines)

For 6 people

600g shoulder of lamb or shin of beef (diced)

250g yellow split peas

3 Large aubergines - cut into circular slices of about 1.5 cm thick

1 Large onion - finely chopped

6 dried Persian limes - soaked and pricked in several places.

2 tbsp. sour grape juice or juice of a lime

1 tsp. turmeric

2 tsp. cinnamon powder

2 tbsp. tomato paste

Salt and pepper for seasoning

Olive or any other pure vegetable oil

A knob of butter

For the Iranian fluffy rice

Ingredients and preparation as per *Chelow* with *Tahdig* (see Chpt.1)

1. Trim & discard any fat around the meat and cut into small 2cm cubes.

2. In a saucepan, fry the chopped onion in a little oil until golden brown and set aside.

3. In the same pan seal the meat, brown and return the onion to the pan. Add the turmeric and cinnamon and give the mixture a stir. Pour over boiling water to form a cover of about 3cm. Stir in the tomato paste. Reduce the heat and simmer for 1 hour 30 minutes or until the meat is tender and fully cooked, stirring occasionally. Half way through cooking add the dried Persian limes, sour grape juice or lime juice and season to taste. If necessary add boiling water to maintain a liquor cover of about 2 cm till the end of cooking.

4. Whilst the *khoresht* is simmering; Pick over the split peas and get rid of any grits or discoloured grains. Wash, dry and then fry lightly for two minutes or so in a little oil. Brush aubergine slices generously with olive oil and cook them for 10 minutes on a griddle or lightly fry, turning them over half way.

5. 20 minutes before serving, add the split peas, butter and give the *Khoresht* a good stir. Place the aubergine slices delicately on top, ensuring that they are covered by 2cm of delicious liquor.

6. For serving, first carefully lift and set aside the aubergines. Empty the casserole (*Khoresht*) into individual bowls and top up with a few aubergine slices. Traditionally the dish is garnished with thinly cut crispy French fries but this is optional.

Serve with *Chelow*, *Tahdig* & your favourite Persian side dish or dishes.

Khoresht-eh Gheymeh Bademjun

(Diced meat stew with aubergines)

Chelow (Iranian fluffy rice) with *Tahdig*

Bademjun (Aubergine)

Perfect for soaking up flavours in stews or curries

CHAPTER 5

Forbidden Fruits & the Secret Service

In Iran and in particular in its capital city Tehran, there were and still are many high schools of a very high standard. Alborz High school where I spent six happy years, if not the best, was one of the top boys' schools.

Shortly after the American civil war ended, many Americans were on the move to foreign destinations. While most were discovering the Wild West, in 1871 a group of missionaries went eastwards. Within two years a school was founded by a group of them headed by Canadian-born, American Presbyterian missionary. This was 33 years before the Constitutional Revolution in Persia. Iran was known as Persia until the reign of Reza Shah (the father of the last Shah of Iran), when it then became known as Iran. Reza Shah changed the name because the Iranian people are of the Aryan race. He believed that this would bring special status to all Persian people; however I and many of my friends still prefer to be called Persian rather than Iranian.

This was the beginning of Alborz High School. While many people played important roles in the history of this magnificent school, two men are well-known, remembered and honoured for its success. Dr. S. Jordan and Dr. M. Mojtahedi.

Dr. Jordan arrived in Persia in 1898. He made various changes and the school became a 12-year elementary and secondary school, offering some college courses. The institution came to be known as the American College of Tehran

During the Second World War, by order of the Reza Shah, as part of his modernization reforms, the school was taken from American management and was put under the Iranian Ministry of Education. At this time the name changed from the American College of Tehran to Alborz High School.

In 1944, Professor Mohammad Ali Mojtahedi, a 33 year old lecturer at the University of Tehran was appointed as the president of Alborz. He was born in

Lahijan Ghilan in the north of Iran and reputedly had a lilting northern accent (*showmali* or *Rashtee*).

I took a lively interest in the school's various extra-curricular activities, and more especially in the end of year celebration gatherings. As a result I was among the students who appeared on stage to entertain the troops, so to speak. I even dared to take the mickey out of Dr Mojtahedi's *showmali* accent and his mannerisms, though as far as I'm aware I didn't offend him.

He used to walk constantly around the yard first thing in the morning and along the long corridors during the breaks, and had an amazing photographic memory for any rule breaking. He used to stop any wrongdoers, take out his little black book and jot down the results of his interrogations. A few "demerits" in the year could lead to a shameful expulsion from the school.

There were about five thousand of us in the school, but Dr Mojtahedi was familiar with both my face and my name. It all started one morning in the first year when I arrived at the school 2 or 3 minutes late. To my horror, he was standing right by the main entrance gate, upright like a sergeant major with a fat Churchill cigar in his mouth. I was summoned. With a grave face, he took his little black book out of his pocket.

"What is your name?" ("*Essmeh shoma*") "Mehrdad Payami" I replied nervously.

"Why are you late Payami?" ("*Chera deer amadii Payami?*") "I'm sorry, I had to take the next bus because my usual bus was packed and I couldn't get on it", I stuttered.

During the rush hour the Sherkateh Vahed buses (Tehran United Bus Company) were indeed jam packed, which would have made London's buses look positively spacious!

Dr Mojtahedi told me that from that day onwards, I should get on three or four buses before my usual one. He then noticed my hair which was fashionably collar length. He grabbed a fistful and pulled it firmly and with a very strong *showmali* accent told me "It must be shortened." ("*Bayad Kaheedeh Shavad.*")

"This event must not be repeated." ("*Teckrar nashavad.*")

The following day Mehrdad Payami, with a much shorter hair style, was the first student to be seen in the school. My obedience, as expected, was noted by the eagle-eyed Dr Mojtahedi who was at the time perambulating in his usual fashion around the yard. I clearly recall his appreciative smile, behind his chunky cigar smoke.

For most of the Twentieth Century, Alborz High School was the premier secondary school for boys in Iran. Its place in the shaping of Iran's intellectual elite, compares with that of Eton in England and Phillips Academy Andover in the United States.

In 1979, the last year of his tenure, Alborz had 5,560 of Iran's best and brightest boy students who were nearly all hand-picked by the Doctor himself.

Dr Mojtahedi was an influential, well respected head and a towering figure in the education of thousands of boys, many of whom went on to some of the world's best colleges and universities. Although I did reasonably well at the school, I was certainly not one of the intellectual elite! I was however very lucky to have attended.

Alborz graduates also made up the core of Iran's post-war young elite, taking every position of power and influence in politics, the health services, universities and corporations.

Dr Mojtahedi had held possibly more prestigious positions, as founder of Aryamehr University (renamed Sharif University after the Islamic Revolution of 1997) and president of several others, in none however, was he as proud and happy as being the principal of Alborz High School.

His ex-students are now spread far and wide, both in Iran and across the world. All these highly educated men of differing backgrounds, religions and political views have three things in common: happy memories; a love for their highly respected high school and an appreciation of the efforts of its charismatic, passionate, yet humble scholar Dr Mojtahedi. I personally remember him for his integrity and unshakable devotion to excellence, something he demanded of himself and his students, and his concern for all our welfare.

After the February 1979 Islamic Revolution, Dr. Mojtahedi found his new circumstances untenable and asked his friend and former colleague, Prime Minister Mehdi Bazargan, to allow him to relinquish his post at Alborz. He passed away on 1 July 1997 in Nice. It has been said that when he was admitted to a hospital in France, he was cared for by doctors and consultants, many of whom were among his ex-students in Tehran. He was buried in Cimetière de l'Est in Nice far from his beloved home.

I understand that Alborz continues to be ranked amongst the best schools in Iran and I'm very proud to be included in its list of past students.

Although we had a very good canteen at the school, some of us preferred to leave the grounds to buy our lunch in one of the nearby fashionable sandwich bars. I used to go to Mobidick or to André, both of which were close to the school. They were very popular, mainly for their delicious chicken salad sandwiches (*Salad-eh-Olivieh*).

It was also well known in the school that the Mobidick was owned by a member of the Royal family.

One day, to avoid a sizeable demonstration gathering outside the Mobidick, I decided to go to André which was about a ten minute walk from the Mobidick. As usual, on the way back to school, I ran to avoid being late only to find myself being entered again into that little black book.

The demonstrators, mainly university students and, as it transpired, members of Iran's Tudeh Party, were ostensibly complaining about a rise in the price of Mobidick sandwiches. However this was a cover and the real reason for the demonstration was a political one.

The Tudeh Party of Iran is a communist party which was formed in 1941. It had considerable influence in its early years and played an important role during Mohammad Mosaddeq's campaign to nationalize the Anglo-Iranian Oil Company during his term as prime minister. Its influence waned in the crackdown that followed the 1953 coup against Mosaddeq. The party still exists today, but is much weaker as a result of the banning of the party and mass arrests by the Islamic Republic in 1982, and the execution of political prisoners in 1988.

The police officers outside the Mobidick were doing all they could to disperse the crowd, using batons and whips. As I was running through the crowd, I was caught across the back of my legs by one of the officers' whips. The force of it knocked me to the pavement. A few seconds later I was able to struggle to my feet and regain my composure. I glanced at the police officer and his leather whip and in order to avoid further trouble calmly walked away.

A few meters away, one of the demonstrators who knew that my father was a colonel, shouted at me "shame on you! Your father is a colonel and you let a less senior officer treat you like an animal? If I were you, I would report him to my dad." In my naivety I turned back, walked towards the officer, noted his name on his badge, gave him a cold smile and a nod and walked away.

A few seconds after this, the officer, accompanied by a second policeman, ran towards me. The officer ordered the policeman to arrest me. They took me to the local police station and to my horror booked me as a destroyer-terrorist (*Mokharreb*). Anti-Shah's activists used to be called *Mokharreb*.

I knew what could happen to someone arrested as a *Mokharreb,* as I had heard many terrible stories. I had personally witnessed the distress of one of my dad's colleagues, whose son had been arrested. His family had not seen their son for over a month, did not know what the boy had done or even where he had been taken for questioning by the secret service. I tried frantically to resist arrest but the policeman hit my wrist hard with his truncheon, smashing my watch to pieces.

The pain and the sight of the broken pieces of my much-loved, gadget watch, brought tears of anger and fear to my eyes. The watch was treasured gift that my brother TJ had given me after returning home from the USA.

I was forcibly taken to the local police station but luckily the same boy who had called "Shame on you…" had seen what had happened and had straightaway passed the news of my arrest to Dr. Mojtahedi's office. The secretary promptly contacted my father. Fortunately my father's office was very close to the police station and before they had a chance to complete their paperwork and arrange my transfer to a security prison, my dad arrived. The door between the room in which I was being held and the reception room was open so I heard my dad's raised voice, demanding to know why on earth his son had been arrested and who had made the arrest.

A few minutes later he came to see me. He walked towards me and at first I thought he was going to hug and comfort me but I was wrong! To my shock, without asking to hear my side of the story, he gave me a hard smack.

I remember hearing a story about a wise old Persian father who asks his son to carry a jug of wine from one end of the room to the other, but before the son has done so, he gives him a hard smack. "Dad, what did you do that for?" the boy asks with tears in his eyes. "Because there will be no point in smacking you after you drop the jug, so be careful my son (*pessaram*)," the father explains.

"How dare you be involved in such a demonstration against the country, and the monarchy and how dare you ruin my good reputation in his majesty's army?" my father shouted.

"I haven't done anything wrong dad and you do not need to worry about your excellent reputation," I replied with a very shaky voice. He then finally let me tell him the full story. As proof, I even handed him the till receipt for my lunch. "Haven't you been told to keep away from demonstrations and haven't you been told that in a fire both dry and wet will eventually burn?" I told dad that I was very sorry and that I shouldn't have gone back to note the officer's name. Although teenagers generally like to keep a safe distance between themselves and their parents, a hug from my father, under the circumstances, would have been much welcomed. He didn't hug me; I had a lesson to learn; to be arrested as a *Mokharreb* was extremely dangerous.

"What's going to happen to me now dad?" I asked. "God knows," he replied. He then left the room swiftly, slamming the door behind him. I was somewhat reassured to hear his raised voice remonstrating with the police officer. A very long half hour later I was released without any formal charge made against me.

I happened to be the students' representative for my class and my short period of absence had been noted by my fellow students and also by the teacher. When I returned to the class everybody looked very concerned and worried but after a few seconds, when they saw the grin of bravado on my face, they all cheered.

Later on, that same day, my dad received a full apology for the incident but unsurprisingly no one offered the poor innocent victim an apology! However when I returned home, my mum and dad's hugs were enough for me.

Although at the time of writing this autobiography, more than forty years has passed since this incident, I can still visualize the senior police officer's face. I know in retrospect that my experience, compared to the experiences of many other innocent individuals, who were wrongfully arrested by the police or the secret service of the time (Savak), is negligible. However, I do wonder what would have happened had my father not been a loyal officer to the late Shah of Iran , perhaps after this incident I could have been influenced by the opposition to the royal family to wrongly blame the Shah as the head of state for this entire incident.

The Mobidick incident was not my only close encounter with the pre-revolutionary Iranian Police or its Secret Service. On two other occasions, again as a totally innocent individual, I had potentially serious encounters with law enforcement.

"Savak" is short for *Sazeman Amneeyat Va Edareh Keshvar* (meaning the Nation's Security & Management Organisation) and each member was called a *Savaki* agent. In the years before the revolution unfortunately many innocent people and their families were subject to brutal, emotional and, according to some people, physical torture and fundamental breaches of their Human Rights. However every nation needs its secret service and not all members of Savak were bad. My father, because of his position in the army, knew a few *Savaki* officers, most of whom were perfectly amiable people. Certainly the atrocities perpetrated by these men pale into insignificance in comparison with the brutality that followed during the revolution of 1979.

On one particular occasion I and a few of my *Alborzi* (meaning from Alborz High School) friends were passing a private clinic, not far from the school. An ambulance suddenly pulled over and my friends and I helped the ambulance crew take a man, who had clearly suffered a gunshot wound into the clinic. The following day we were passing the same clinic, and we naively asked the receptionist if the poor man had recovered from the gunshot wound. She gave us a very suspicious look and answered "which poor man?" We told her not to worry and quickly left.

We were about fifty meters or so away when one of my friends told us that he felt uncomfortable about the situation and that we should run away as fast as we could. At the same time two men, who later proved to be *Savaki*, rushed out of the clinic and shouted to us to stop at once.

We were nearly at a 'T' junction so my friends decided to turn left and make a run for it. I however decided to stop, turn back and walk towards the men. God knows what would have happened to us all if I, like the others had done a runner!

I was arrested and taken inside the clinic. They took me to a cold and very quiet room for questioning. First they asked my name, address, and what I'd been doing, then they left me, quaking with terror, in that room alone and went to check the accuracy of the information I'd given. After an hour or so they returned and continued their interrogation.

"How did you know a wounded man was brought here yesterday?"

"Because I was among the people who helped the poor man into the clinic," I replied.

"The man was stabbed by a drug dealer, during a deal which went wrong. What made you to mention a shot gun wound?"

'There was no stabbing sir;' I replied with a shaky voice.

"Oh, really, you know better? What makes you so sure? Were you there when it all happened?"

"No sir. The man was wearing a white shirt and if he was stabbed one would expect to see a cut through his shirt and anyway the pattern of bleeding indicated a shotgun wound".

"Who do you think you are? Detective Colombo or a forensic expert?

"No Sir I have watched many John Wayne western movies and I know about gunshot wounds;" I replied naively.

"Enough of this nonsense. Tell us the truth or you will be in deep shit boy."

"Honestly sirs please believe me, I'm telling you the truth and when I look back I shouldn't have offered my help to the ambulance crew"

"Why did the people you were with run away?

"I don't know. Perhaps they were scared of being arrested."

My refusal to provide them with the surnames of my friends increased their suspicion and prolonged their interrogation. I asked if they would allow me to phone home, which they refused.

They took a few mug shots and left me in the cold locked room for a further two hours. When they returned they informed me that they had evidence of my presence at the scene of the drug deal and that if I wanted less harsh punishment I should tell them my full involvement in all of this. I think they were just testing my reaction to this accusation.

"Punishment? Punishment for what sir? For helping the ambulance crew carry an injured person?" I complained, my voice shaking and tears welling up in my eyes. I told them that there was nothing else I could add to my statement and that they should check with my school for proof that I was in a classroom at the time of incident.

They left the room again and returned after a few more interminable hours. They then told me that the ambulance crew had actually confirmed my story about helping them and that they were going to release me without making any formal charges. As in my previous brush with the Savak, there was no apology for my unjustified arrest and interrogation.

I was supposed to return home soon after the school closed and knew that my parents would be frantic with worry. My friends could have contacted my parents, but they were only school friends and they knew neither our home number, nor where I lived.

After leaving the clinic, I immediately called home from a telephone box and told my very worried dad about the arrest and how sorry I was to cause them such worry again. When I eventually returned home, it was well after dusk. My poor parents were delighted to see me. I first jokingly asked my dad not to smack me! And then once again felt assured and relaxed as they hugged me in relief.

For at least several days after this incident, a guy (presumably a Savaki) followed me like a shadow everywhere I went. The situation was very worrying but eventually, presumably realising that they were dealing with an innocent but naive teenager, the surveillance stopped.

I have many great memories, some more embarrassing than others, of my teenage innocence. One of my treasured memories is that of my summer holidays in the lush green resorts of the southern shore of the Caspian Sea.

As mentioned in a previous chapter, my father received a number of great perks as a colonel. One of these was the use of a villa, which we took advantage of once or twice a year. Situated in a very well-kept and pleasant seaside resort, called Noshahr (meaning New City) it was used exclusively by Iranian and American army officers. Noshahr was located about 6 kilometres to the east of the Caspian seaside town of Chaloos on the northern side of the Alborz Mountain.

The camp had a massive swimming pool, a big jetty (which was the site of many a romantic encounter among visitors to Noshahr), a huge blissfully cool, multi-functional hall called the Blue Hall (*Talar-eh-Abi*), twenty or so villas for senior army officers, a handful of exclusive villas for use by US military officers and their families, and many tents and marquees for the junior officers. It even had its own runway which as far as I'm aware was for the exclusive use of the Royal family and top ranking officers.

It was known that the Shah of Iran had a villa not far from the resort, and I actually recall being overwhelmed by seeing a very young crown prince of Iran just the other side of a metal fence, which formed a low lying boundary between the resort and its runway. Although Prince Reza, who now lives in America, at the time was no more than six years or so old, his mannerisms were very adult. He came towards me and gave a nice smile and a wave before being put in a limousine, possibly to join his parents.

The sea was clean but the water was often cloudy because of the waves and the very salty sea-bed. As a result it was often difficult to spot the turtles, various types of fish including sturgeon and other sea creatures that were plentiful in its waters. During these holidays I would spend many hours in the clearer water of the rivers at the estuaries, catching turtles, water snakes and even sometimes to my horror being attacked by a group of fresh water leeches.

One day all of a sudden the sea became very rough, almost as though a minor tsunami was about to happen. Within the section of the shore that lifeguards patrolled, a woman was happily enjoying the sea with her two toddlers. As the height of the waves suddenly increased it became clear that the poor woman and her toddlers (one under each arm) were in trouble. Other swimmers too were calling for help and there weren't enough lifeguards to assist all of them at the same time.

As I was resting on a raised platform I could clearly see what was happening, so I dived in and swam as quickly as I could towards the woman with her children. Grabbing her legs I lifted her up above the water line and with my own head under the water began to walk towards the shore. Finally all three were lifted away from me out of the water. I must have been under the water for quite some time, as I soon discovered that I too needed rescuing. I was so lucky that the rescued woman had asked one of the lifeguards to search for me as well. I am still proud that I, as a young teenager, managed to save all three of them that day.

The fresh water swimming pool at the resort was massive, about 100m long by 20m wide. One day, as usual after swimming in the sea, I went there to swim and to wash the salt off my body. Unlike other days, on this day the swimming pool was absolutely empty and there were two army guards standing outside the entrance gate. Suddenly a black limousine pulled up, the chauffeur opened the door and a man a bit older than my father got out and walked towards the swimming pool. I thought the pool was just about to be opened so I walked in behind this man.

When the man approached the pool, the guards saluted and immediately opened the gates and to my surprise as I followed him in they shut the gates quickly behind me. I could not go back out so I said hello to the man and went to the far end of the pool and enjoyed a swim, whilst the man stayed at the other end of the pool.

A little while later, as I left the pool alone having had my swim, the guards began to realise that I had nothing to do with this man and was not related to him; clearly they should not have let me in. They then informed me that I'd had the pleasure of swimming alone in the pool with Arteshbod Bahram Aryana, the country's top 4 star general!

I realised that he must have been an important person, but I would never have guessed that he was the Shah's top general. Surprisingly the general didn't make any fuss and let me enjoy the pool. He could have had me kicked out and that might have been yet another encounter with our national security forces!

As they say in Farsi: *Ta seh nasheh bazee nasheh;* that roughly translates to: 'Until there are three we cannot play'. In other words things happen in three's. Whilst writing about Noshahr, I may as well tell you the story of my third close encounter with the national security forces and of my first amorous escapade!

Our week's holiday at the resort had ended and we had to hand over the villa to another family and leave the camp. Although during this stay I'd managed to make some new friends and had really enjoyed myself, I missed the friends that I'd met the previous year, very much.

All dishes that were served to us in the blue hall were tasty and mouth-watering, but their diced meat stew with aubergines (*Khoresht-eh Gheymeh Bademjun*) was undoubtedly my favourite. I asked my parents if we could have a quick lunch there before going back home, and whilst there, to my delight, my friends from the previous year suddenly appeared. They were just starting their holiday, so for the first time in my life I dared ask my parents if they would trust me enough to let me stay behind to enjoy yet another week at the resort. My father asked where I would be sleeping and I replied without hesitation that there would be no problem, as there were many cheap simple bamboo huts for rent just outside the camp. I promised that I wouldn't under any circumstances swim beyond the boundary line of the safe allocated section of the sea, and wouldn't swim at all when the flag on the beach was not green.

It just happened that our family dentist and his rather attractive wife Setareh (meaning a star in Persian) had a villa just outside the camp, so before agreeing to let me stay behind, Mum and Dad had decided to ask them if they would keep an eye on me if I needed any help. The dentist was working in Tehran but his wife was spending a few weeks there alone. I later found out that they were having some marital problems. She told my parents that she would be happy to look out for me and that I was welcome to sleep at the villa anytime. Her kind offer reassured my parents and, having provided me with some more pocket money to cover the cost of my stay and the coach fare home, they left me behind.

That night, after the Blue Hall had closed, and having spent an hour or so on the romantically lit jetty, I arrived back at the villa sometime after midnight. I used the key that Setareh had given me and let myself into the villa, assuming that she would be asleep. She was not in, so I went to bed in one of the spare rooms.

Just before 4am, Setareh appeared in my room, bent over my body flicking her beautiful long, wet hair over me to wake me up. She was wearing a very thin white shirt that didn't leave much to the imagination. Was I dreaming, was I Dustin Hoffman in The Graduate? Setareh smiled at me enigmatically and asked me to come down to the beach with her. "The sea, when it's raining, just before dawn is very peaceful and an experience you won't forget," she said in a husky voice.

She was absolutely right about the tranquillity of the sea. She didn't bother to change into her swimsuit, took hold of my hand and dragged me, wearing just my underpants into the sea. She put her arms around my shoulders and started kissing me! I was shocked. She was a married woman, married to my dentist of all things! Somehow my shock overcame my erm … other reactions and I pushed her away. I know she was happy, but why she behaved like she did I have no idea. Perhaps she was drunk I thought.

We went back to the villa and I returned resolutely to the spare room. Next morning to prevent any further embarrassment, I decided to tell her that my friends had asked me to stay in their villa and that I wouldn't be disturbing her any further. She agreed that if it was okay with my parents it would be fine with her as well. However, I hadn't asked my friends if they had room for me, and I soon found that, as it was high season, all the bamboo huts were taken. Luckily I discovered that one of the tents at the resort was unoccupied. I got myself a locker, stored my belongings and used the tent only to sleep for the rest of my stay. And I did indeed have a great time with my old friends.

I have one more tale to tell about what happened on the last night of my stay in the camp.

As on previous nights, I returned to my tent a few hours after midnight, but on this occasion, to my disbelief, I found it was now occupied by a family. I didn't feel I could stay in the area, as it might draw the attention of the guards and then I might face awkward questions or look a bit foolish, so I decided to leave.

Bedding down on the grass verge outside the camp or along the road would also have attracted either the army guards or local police officers, so I decided the best thing would be to walk to the nearest town and get back to camp just before dawn. Wearing a pair of cotton shoes and holding a long torch in my hand, I set off.

Just before I reached Chaloos which was about 6km from the camp, I noticed a few rather expensive looking villas which were set back a few meters from the road. There were a handful of people on the balcony of one of these villas, socialising and enjoying themselves. Outside there was a row of citrus trees laden with fruits. I approached the trees with arm extended and my torch in hand, I located a few fruits that could be easily reached.

Just as I was about to pick a juicy orange a voice shouted out "Stop, stop" (*East, East*). I quickly backed off but was instantly surrounded by two uniformed policemen and three plain clothes officers (in all likelihood secret service). One of the guys asked me where I had dropped the weapon. "Weapon? Which weapon?" I answered my heart racing. "The weapon that was in your hand, targeting that balcony" he said.

I told them the entire story, now feeling somewhat foolish. After some more questioning they let me go, but told me that I would be closely followed all the way to Chaloos and back to the camp. They made it very clear that any further suspicious behaviour on my part and things would not go well for me.

One of the police officers did indeed follow me very closely all the way back to the camp. I was hungry and all the shops except for a fruit store were closed at that time, so I bought a kilo of plums. I turned and offered the bag to the police officer, and he quickly jammed one into his mouth and spat out the stone. I asked him what all the business on the balcony had been about; as it seemed by this time he began to trust me and believed my story.

"You see, important members of the royal family (he hinted perhaps even the Shah himself) were socialising on that balcony, and your posture with your arm raised facing the balcony made us believe that you were just about to shoot someone." I realised then how lucky I'd been, that I hadn't got into more serious trouble, and resolved at that point to be much more careful in future.

When we arrived at the camp, the fact that the guards at the entrance obviously knew me confirmed to him that my story was indeed true. We shook hands and he headed back.

The situation with Setareh had made me keenly aware that I ought to do something on the girl friend front. However having a sexual relationship in Iran before marriage, even before the Islamic Revolution was generally much frowned upon by most people. Girls were expected to be virgins on their wedding night. This was somewhat unfair on the boys, and the girls too I suspect!

One friend, Ali Reza, who I used to play volleyball with, was rather ahead of me in this respect. He understood, man to man, my predicament. One evening, (as my favourite Scottish comedian Kevin Bridges says) when he had "an empty" (meaning his Mum and Dad were out!) he orchestrated an encounter for me. His parents were away for the weekend, so had taken the opportunity to invite myself and an acquaintance of his, Mina, over to his place. I wasn't aware of Ali Reza's plan and didn't realise that he would immediately leave the two of us alone!

Mina, who was actually rather attractive, turned out to be, for want of a better word, a concubine. She was happy to accommodate 'decent' boys that she found attractive, for some kind of financial assistance. So she would, for example welcome a nice pair of shoes, a hand bag, perfume etc. or just be content being taken out for a nice meal.

I hope you won't think this is in poor taste, but Mina left the room and re-appeared a short time later dressed as a nurse! A rather sexy nurse if the truth be told. Apparently Ali Reza had told her of my virgin state and even more embarrassingly of my fondness for nurses in short uniforms. She'd come well prepared!

Returning to the main story again, my six years at Alborz High School were soon over and I had to make a decision about my future academic studies. My two brothers Iradj & Touradj (TJ) were both studying at university overseas and my parents used their savings to send money on a regular basis to pay for their education and living expenses. Since an army officers' salary was relatively low, Mum and Dad's financial situation at that time wasn't good.

On one occasion, much to his surprise, my father was approached directly by the head of Savak (General Naseeri) to see if he would consider undertaking additional national security duties. He told the general that unfortunately his morals and his faith (Baha'i) wouldn't allow him to be involved with the Secret Service. However we knew a few non Baha'i officers who, after accepting a similar offer, found their financial situation and their general lifestyle had changed for the better.

One of Dad's duties in the army was to recommend suitable colonels to the Shah's top generals for promotion. Dad felt that it was time now for him to seek promotion, to improve his financial circumstances. However, even though it would have been well-deserved, the promotion did not materialise.

From a security point of view the Shah trusted and liked Baha'is very much. I believe the family's doctor was specially chosen because he was a Baha'i. However, the Mullahs, who were and still are, vehemently against Baha'is, had considerable influence over the structure of the armed forces. Furthermore a number of Muslim generals who held more strict beliefs (and interestingly who ended up betraying the Shah during the revolution of 1979) were strongly opposed to the promotion of officers who were followers of the Baha'i Faith.

One of the generals, who knew my dad well, was at that time responsible for a special section of the Armed Forces, the Gendarmerie. He was aware of my father's financial position, so he kindly informed my dad that there would be a non-political vacancy there for him. My father thought that if he was allowed to retire as a colonel, he could start a new post in the Gendarmerie as a plain clothes senior officer, thereby boosting his income. The new job mainly involved teaching other officers military tactics for the general management of the country and its national security (*Neeroyeh Payehdari Va Edareh Keshvar*).

My dad's application for early retirement failed several times, but eventually he was made redundant and was appointed to the new job straight away. Though slightly improved, his salary still wasn't high.

A lot of middle class families at that time, sent their children to Europe or America to complete their further education. However, this was a costly enterprise and since my parents were supporting my elder brothers, in Austria and America, they had sacrificed a lot to do so. As a result I reckoned the best thing for me to do would be to join the armed forces.

Joining the Royal Navy as an Engineer Officer appealed to me very much for various reasons. One was that I would have the opportunity to travel the world. I understood that the Shah's Royal Navy had a base in Portsmouth, England. (As an aside, apparently after the revolution the entire crew of an Iranian battleship moored at Portsmouth, mutinied and refused to sail their ship back home.)

The second was that the Royal Navy and the Shah's other armed forces were among the best in the world, and I wanted to have the privilege of serving the country that I loved so much.

The third was that girls might fancy me in a military or police uniform! Surely girls with good taste must fancy Navy officers in their white uniforms?

It took me over three months to complete all the necessary medical and academic exams. I found the medicals, which included an assessment of the applicants' ability to be calm in stressful situations, a bit nerve racking, but the academic exams were relatively easy. Having passed both of these successfully, within a week I received a letter from the Navy, informing me that I had been accepted, providing joining details and a starting date.

One day, before I received the letter from the Royal Navy, I had explained to my friend, Hooman, the main reason for my wanting to join up, to avoid burdening my parents with further expense. Without realising the consequences, Hooman mentioned this to her mother, who promptly told my mother.

My parents always wanted to treat their children exactly the same and were saddened by my actions and therefore decided that like my brothers, I too should go abroad to complete my higher education, with a view to returning home afterwards to work. I resisted strongly, but they were determined. Going to the USA would be very expensive and financially impossible for my dad. Going to Austria and joining my other brother was not a good idea either, because I couldn't speak a word of German. So it was decided that England would be the destination for me.

Dad (far left), during the 1953 coup in Iran

Dad (far right), whilst working for the *Neeroyeh Payehdari*

To a teenager, picking these juicy citrus fruits at

three in the morning is tempting, but at what cost!

Alborz High School – 1974

Patriotic songs by Alborzi students (2500 years celebration of the Persian Empire)

Happy School Days

Alborz High School- 1974

Proud to be an Alborzi

Salad-eh-Olivieh

(Iranian chicken & potato salad)

For 6 people - as an appetizer

A pair of skinless chicken breast fillets

6 medium sized waxy potatoes

6 large free range eggs

100g of frozen garden peas

4 medium size gherkins

About 6 tbsp. of good quality egg mayonnaise. (I use Hellman's Real Mayo)

1 tsp. of lemon juice

Salt & white pepper – About 1 tsp. of each

1tbsp extra virgin olive oil

Baguette slices, Pita bread, Vol-au-vent shells or Iranian bread (*Bar Bari*) which can be found in Turkish food stores.

1. Peel and boil the potatoes until cooked. Hard boil the eggs and when the potatoes and eggs are cool chop finely or grate with a large grater.

2. Meanwhile cook the garden peas for a few minutes only so they are still bright green and firm and set aside to cool.

3. Put the chicken in a pot. Add water just to cover the chicken and bring to a rapid boil. Season and simmer on low heat for 20 minutes till fully cooked. Set aside to cool.

4. Dice the chicken into 1cm cubes, finely chop the gherkins and put all the ingredients into a large bowl. Add the mayo, lemon juice and the extra virgin olive oil. Mix thoroughly, taste and add more seasoning if necessary. Personally I like adding quite a bit of diced gherkin to give the dish a little note of sharpness, but this is a matter of taste.

Serving suggestions:

As a canapé, small individual portions on side plates with bread or on a platter decorated with any combination of grated cooked eggs, garden peas, and/or pitted black olives. Some people use a topping layer of mayo and a combination of the above as garnishing but I prefer not to.

Note: Apparently *Salad-eh Olivieh* was originally invented in the 1860s by a Russian chef of Belgian origin called Lucien Olivier. He worked for the *Hermitage* (one of Moscow's most celebrated restaurants). However unlike the above recipe, one of the ingredients of the Russian version is diced cooked carrots. Adding carrots makes the dish a bit sweet for me so I, and indeed almost all Iranians leave it out.

Salad-eh -Olivieh (Iranian chicken & potato salad)

A legend never dies

Dr Mojtahedi & I (1973)

CHAPTER 6

Platform Shoes & Cheesecloth Shirts

After staying in Hannah's homely house for two years, it was time for me to move on. Chani's large Victorian house, with its initially grimy and rather basic loft space bedsit, gave me the total freedom and privacy that, I was missing at Hannah's.

Chani treated me like a younger brother rather than a tenant and he took me under his wing, just as Hannah had. I must have looked as though I needed mothering, or brothering. He would invite me to join him in having delicious meals with his very kind wife and two charming daughters, and would assist me whenever I needed his help. I was very lucky, but I guess I was also an easy going and respectful tenant. Many of my friends had endless problems with their landlords.

The bed that Chani provided me with, though comfortable, had rather squeaky springs. I didn't want to make a fuss, so I just placed the mattress directly on the floor and stored the components of the frame in a storage space under the eaves. In that space, I confess, I also put a few of the more rickety or less tasteful items of furniture and covered over my mattress, table and the skylight with matching oriental looking Persian fabric. I also bought a few large cushions to go on the mattress and covered these with the same fabric.

I added a few posters on the walls (I look back and cringe at what I then thought was cool!), rearranged the remaining furniture and placed a few candles and Persian handmade ornaments here and there. Before I knew it, I had converted a cold somewhat grim loft space into a warm cosy bedsit.

That summer, as I had for the past two years, I travelled to Iran to visit my family. By then I was clean-shaven with proper 1970's long hair resting on my shoulders. I was wearing much more fashionable clothes than when I arrived in the UK. I'm talking about a pair of tight fitting, stonewashed Levi vintage 501's, a slim fit denim Levi jacket over a slim fit (I note the 'slim-fit' with despair now!) striped cheesecloth shirt and a pair of platform shoes. I also wore a leather necklace with a metallic peace sign pendant, and of course I had liberally sprinkled my body with the latest version of Brut aftershave by Fabergé.

During the early 70's, young men's fashion adopted a look that would have been considered too feminine in the 60's, but by the end of the 70's, the fashion trend changed again and the punks rejected everything that had gone before. However the punk look just didn't do it for me. Sad though it sounds, part of me still harks back to the 70's as my sartorial spiritual home. Well what goes around comes around, and I'm sure bell bottoms will be back.

At Heathrow, whilst waiting for my flight to Tehran, I found myself standing next to a very tall, well known gentleman. I looked up, raising my chin by some 90 degrees, and stared fascinated at the long lean jaw and aquiline nose. Like many in the terminal building I recognised him immediately. "Hello" I said, as though I'd known him for years, and he returned my hello with his glittering eyes and a familiar grin, showing his sharp shiny canine teeth. These teeth appeared to lengthen and I shivered. It was, as you may have already guessed, the most famous Dracula actor Christopher Lee. For several nights afterwards I awoke in a cold sweat clutching my neck!

I was no longer the nerdy teenager I had been on my first flight to the UK, and soon got chatting with the air hostesses. I was more self-assured and, I like to think, a little more mature, not to mention more fashionably attired! I didn't need to ask the hostesses for endless refreshments just to create the opportunity for a chat. I guess because I was more confident they responded to that, and seemed to want to converse with me. Although I was getting better in the fine art of flirting, I still found chatting-up British girls challenging. Their minds were a complete mystery to me and I could never really read what they were feeling.

On this particular flight, I established a rapport with three of the female members of the crew! Iran Air (before the revolution of 1979), employed both Iranian and non-Iranians as air crew. One of these was Sal.

It was Sal's and the other two hostess' first trip to Iran, and they had a few days off staying in Tehran, before flying back to London. Naturally, as guests of my country, I wanted them to thoroughly enjoy their stay.

Despite negative western perceptions (largely because of the hostage crisis and then the revolution) Persians are generally known, both by visitors to Iran and by their non-Iranian friends abroad, to be warm and hospitable people. We take our traditional role as hosts and representatives of our nation very seriously indeed. This is deep in the national psyche and extends without prejudice to all nationalities and beliefs.

In order to enhance these three guests' short visit, I offered them my own hospitality. I agreed to pick them up each day from their hotel and take them sight-seeing, not only to the more touristy places in the capital, but also to less well known sights, and some of the countryside surrounding Teheran. Tehran like Athens has many interesting places to visit, but some of these are difficult to find without a guide.

As a capital city of a vast country, Teheran was and still is over-crowded and highly polluted, especially during the summer, with the temperature sometimes soaring to well over 40 degrees. The heat, the sheer volume of traffic, the hugely inefficient public transport system, coupled with all the signs being in Farsi made navigating one's way around the city, without a Persian guide, tricky to say the least. So the acceptance of my offer by Sal and her friends came as no surprise.

Western people, back in the Shah's time, regarded the Iranians as very rich (*kheylee pooldar*), and they could see this demonstrated in the daily lives of the country's elite, that were on student visas in the West. Even if they're not rich, Persians do like to put on a good show. This can mean in the classic British phrase "all fur coat and no knickers" - see here the mastery of my adopted culture's idioms! So I think Sal and her friends were understandably expecting me to turn up in a Porsche or Lamborghini! The day after our arrival, I turned up outside their hotel in an Iranian built sport version of the Hillman Hunter (*Peykan-eh Javanan*). It was lime green and boasted tinted windows and alloy wheels. If they were disappointed they certainly didn't show it!

We escaped the heat, traffic, and pollution of the city and headed north into the mountains, welcoming the mountain breeze which funnelled through the green valleys. To extend my hospitality further, I took them to our house for some refreshments.

The next day we toured the sites of Tehran, but Sal's friends became very tired after lunch, so I took them back to their hotel early that afternoon. Sal however seemed fine, so as previously agreed with my parents; I took her back home to have a dinner with my family.

Mum had planned the dinner as a bit of surprise for us both, because it turned out that many other members of my family had also been invited. I felt so sorry for poor Sal, meeting a big contingent of my family unexpectedly. However things worked out well, even if did feel a bit uncomfortable. All the younger members of my family were well-educated and could converse in English reasonably well. The conversation flowed easily with even the elder members trying to communicate with gestures and lots of yeses, nos and maybes, just as I had done on my first day in the UK!

Sal appeared very relaxed and seemed to enjoy the attention that my family was giving her. A number of the older members of the family even asked me if marriage with her was in the air!

Mum served her a delicious beef stew cooked with celery (*Khoreshteh Karafse*) with fluffy saffron rice and potato *tahdig*. It was a memorable meal and I have shared her recipe with you at the end of this chapter!

Sal and I got on very well together. She was genuine, charming and pretty. During her stay in Tehran I did try to ... erm... get off with her, without success, though we did remain very amicable, so I couldn't have been too crass! To me at that time, being just good friends with a girl, particularly an attractive one, was beyond my comprehension. Although Sal had a boyfriend in London, she was not averse to the odd kiss, but nothing more. A form of torture I reckon, but character building I hope!

A few months after my return to England I received a phone call from Sal, asking to meet her in a pub, explaining that she would like to return my hospitality in kind. I was very happy to hear from her and although I was supposed to meet some friends that evening, I knew they'd understand.

It was wonderful seeing Sal again. We went to a wine bar and the conversation flowed effortlessly. When I asked about her boyfriend she told me that it was all over. I didn't know whether to grin or to try to be sympathetic.

As the evening went on, hoping to advance my cause, I made my first and only foray into poetry. I recited one of Omar Khayyam's poems that has been translated here into English by Edward Fitzgerald.

Ah, fill the cup, what boots it to repeat.
How time is slipping underneath our Feet.
Unborn tomorrow, and dead yesterday.
Why fret about them if today be sweet!

I told my wife this story some thirty three years after the event and she commented that the Scottish version of this Persian poem (*Ruba'i*) is probably summarised with the phrase "Yer a long time deed (dead)!"

Near closing time, I asked Sally back to my place for coffee.

My room was a bit cold, so I offered her the cardigan I was wearing. The light in my room was rather bright and harsh, so thinking myself a smooth operator, I told her that I'd run out of 5p coins for the meter, which gave me a good excuse to light a few candles. However, the room was so cold that after a while huddled shivering together on the cushions, surprise, surprise I managed to find a coin to turn on the heating.

We sat next to each other on the mattress, lounging against two large cushions. The atmosphere of the room reminded Sal of the traditional tea houses in Iran. We chatted for a while and then she asked me if she could stay the night. However, before anything could happen she burst into tears. It turned out that she was still mourning the break up with her boyfriend, so I comforted her as best I could, with all thoughts of furthering our relationship now abandoned, much to my disappointment!

In the morning I made her breakfast, after which she gave me a big kiss and a hug and left, appearing much more cheerful. Somehow, I was hoping that she might phone after a few days, to tell me that she'd changed her mind and wanted to see me again. However, a few months later, I received a phone call from a very happy Sally, advising that thanks to me, she had reunited with her boyfriend and that they were now engaged. I was happy for her, but still occasionally wonder what might have been.

A few weeks after Sal's call, I met a sweet baby faced Irish girl called Sharon. She had a lovely, gentle southern Irish accent. Sharon and I got on well, and she became my first proper and steady girlfriend. Our relationship lasted several months. However, after a while Sharon wanted things to become more serious. I was focused on completing my studies and wasn't really ready to make this kind of commitment. As tactfully as I could, I told her this.

To my horror she burst into tears and ran out of the house. I was so worried about the extremity of her reaction, that I quickly followed, and saw her disappear into her bedsit, just around the corner. After I had rung her bell countless times, eventually one of the other tenants in the house opened the main door. I knocked repeatedly on her door, but couldn't get her to answer. Since I knew she was in there, this total silence caused me great alarm.

Finding my way into the rear garden, I forced the back door, and eventually managed to get into her bedsit. I found her tearfully sitting on the bed, extremely pale, shivering and totally silent. It took a moment or two before I noticed with horror the blood dripping from her tightly clasped hands. In total panic I phoned 999. Had I not gone after her or not found my way into her bedsit, those thoughts remained with me for many months afterwards.

We did remain friends, but I was extremely wary. I tried to support her as best I could, and she eventually travelled back to Ireland six months later. I heard subsequently from her sister that she was much happier back home.

I decided to have a break from dating for quite a while after this incident.

My next foray into dating was Ládan. Ládan was a Persian girl, who I'd met in Iran just before coming to the UK. We met at a gathering in Tehran, that was arranged especially for students on their way to foreign soil. The students were expected, by both their family and the regime, to return home after finishing their higher education. The country in the late 60's and early 70's was undergoing rapid modernisation, it needed and indeed expected its well-educated elite to return home to assist with this modernisation plan. After all, in order to work towards the great civilisation, which was planned by the Shah's regime, the input of each individual soul, especially each western-educated individual was required.

Whilst in Iran, Ládan and I found out, coincidently, not only were we both going to London, we were also heading for the same college. We felt relieved that we would know someone on foreign soil, and especially that we'd be living and studying quite near each other. However, for some reason Ládan went to another college first, to study English, before turning up a year or so later at my college. Since I was there well before her and was familiar with the amenities, I became a very handy person to know.

Whilst writing about Ládan, how can I not tell you about my dear friend Amir? Amir was my first friend in London. I have never forgotten what he (aka Mr Casanova) did to me, only a few months after becoming my friend.

One day, whilst Amir and I were half way through our canteen lunch, Ládan materialised. Shortly after being introduced to Amir, Ládan suddenly realised that she needed to be in another building to register her name for a course. She didn't know the whereabouts of this building and asked if I could accompany her. "No problem, just let me have a few seconds to finish my plate Ládan" I said. But before I was able to take my next forkful 'Mr Casanova' had downed the rest of his lunch at break neck speed and offered to escort her in my stead. I have never seen anybody eat so quickly in my whole life, and I sincerely hope he suffered severe indigestion. Ládan was in such a rush that she accepted his offer without hesitation. I sat there completely dumbfounded.

The morning after his escapade, Mr Casanova had the nerve to describe to me in some detail, escorting Ládan home on the train and giving her a passionate kiss as they went through a tunnel. How I have remained friends with Amir for the last 40 years is a mystery to me!

Although I didn't brood over Amir's betrayal, I wasn't going to let him to get away with it that easily. The next day we were having lunch in the canteen when again Ládan joined us, and after a very warm greeting for Amir, she acknowledged my existence with cool politeness. I knew that Ládan would be annoyed if she found out that Amir had told me about their private moment on the train, so the stage was set! I quoted her a well-known Persian phrase. "*No keh áyad be bazaar- koh neh shavad del ázaar.*" This means 'when something new comes to the bazaar the old stuff losses its appeal'. Well, she sent Amir a thunderous look and from then on kept her distance from him. After that episode, her attention returned to me but I don't like coming second, so shortly after that Ládan moved on. I secretly hoped she'd realise what she'd lost!

Amir, I and later on another fellow student called Freydoon became very firm friends. We three musketeers went clubbing and chasing girls every weekend, and had great fun doing so.

Freydoon, just like Amir, turned out to be another smooth operator, so charming that girls would feel immediately at ease with him. He was Mr Casanova 2. His English was so bad that even we used to take the micky. However, it seemed his appalling English worked very well for him, and the girls like Brigit, as he used to call her "Brie-sheet", were easily charmed. His character was reminiscent of Costas in the 1989 film, "Shirley Valentine", though I'm not sure if he ever asked a girl if she want to make f**ky with him. I wouldn't entirely have put it past him.

However poor Freydoon had one very strange attribute. Dogs absolutely hated him. Whenever a dog came near, it would bark frantically and launch itself at the hapless Freydoon. Although we found this hilarious, Freydoon did not see the funny side and eventually came to believe that British dogs were prejudiced against him! Freydoon sadly never really settled in London and before completing his studies, packed his suitcase and went back home for good.

After finishing his A 'levels Amir betrayed me again, at least that's what I thought at the time. He decided that he was going to Southampton to do a Chemical Engineering degree. I was devastated to lose both him and Freydoon. "Out of sight out of mind" I thought sadly. I fully expected the friendship to fizzle out, but this proved not to be the case, and we carried on seeing each other from time to time, either in Southampton or London.

Don't you just love my platform shoes?

1970's - Anything Goes Days   *Fever night, fever night, fever*

Khoresht-eh Karafse

(Beef stew with celery and mint)

For 6 people

600g shin of beef- diced

6 large celery sticks - cut into batons

1 Large onion - finely chopped

2 tbsp. sour grape juice or juice of a lime

6 dried Persian limes soaked/pricked

1 tsp. turmeric

2 tsp. cinnamon powder

A bunch of fresh mint leaves (finely chopped) or 2 tbsp. dried mint (soaked & then drained)

Salt and pepper for seasoning

Olive or any other pure vegetable oil

A large knob of butter

For the Iranian fluffy rice

Ingredients and preparation as per *Chelow* with *Tahdig* (see Chpt.1)

1. Trim & discard any fat around the meat and cut into small 2cm cubes.

2. In a saucepan, fry the chopped onion and celery in 3 tablespoons of oil for about two minutes. Add the mint towards the end of frying and set aside.

3. Seal the diced beef in the same saucepan. Return the chopped onion, celery and mint to the pan. Add the turmeric and cinnamon and give the *khoresht* mixture a good stir. Pour over boiling water to form a cover of about 3cm. Reduce heat and simmer, stirring gently from time to time and if necessary add boiling water to maintain a liquor cover of about 2 cm till the end of cooking.

4. After about 45 minutes add the sour grape juice, dried limes, butter and season to taste. Simmer gently for further 45 minutes or so till the meat is tender and fully cooked.

5. Serve with *Chelow* and *Tahdig* (Chpt. 1) & your favourite side dish/es.

Khoresht-eh Karafse (Beef Stew with celery and mint)

1977- Our brand new Peykan-eh Javanan

(Iraninan built Sport Hillman Hunter)

CHAPTER 7

The Trouble Maker

The absence of my good friend Amir, and the lack of any other real companionship, had a significant effect on me. I had many other friends at college, but at that time, when Amir decided to go to Southampton, I was not as close to any of them as I was to Mr Casanova. I recall staying indoors alone in the evenings, listening to sad, traditional Persian music, looking at old black & white photographs, feeling more and more homesick and depressed. After returning home from college, I would try hard to cheer myself up with home-cooked food, and every day I would make a Persian dish. I even learnt to cook one of my favourite recipes, mixed herb rice with lamb shank and broad beans (*Baghali Polo ba Mahicheh*). However even after eating this, it didn't really cheer me up, as it is well known that "manly" eating does make the diner feel a little heavy and tired.

One evening, thoughts of the good old days and of the void, that the loss of both Mr Casanovas had left, really got me down. In addition, after my experience with Sharon, I'd had a good few months break from dating, so I was feeling more than a little lonely. I thought that instead of cooking and eating at home, going to the night spot where curly Barbara and I used to work, would cheer me up.

I didn't want to go there alone so I contacted a few friends to accompany me. Unfortunately, they were either not in or had other commitments, so I ended up going on my own. As a previous employee I knew the required dress code, so I went very smartly dressed. I was wearing a pair of well-polished black shoes, formal black trousers and had on my favourite shirt, a very nice light grey silk shirt with white pinstripes that I'd bought from an exclusive Bond Street menswear shop.

£29.99 was the price that I paid for that shirt. When I look back I must have been mad, as a poor student to pay such a high price for a shirt. Who did I think I was? The Prince of Persia! It was a lot of money back in 1977 to pay for a shirt. To be frank, all of the shirts that I now wear after 40 years or so as a professional person have been purchased for under £29.99 each. Perhaps with the passing of the time, I have become meaner or simply a wiser person.

I got to the club early and at the front door there were a few doormen, none of whom were familiar to me. Some doormen used to be very cocky with customers that they didn't like the look of. So sometimes, to take revenge, the victims used to return after a few weeks. This meant that, in order to avoid being hurt, the bouncers within a given area were always swapping their places of work.

I was at the front of the queue and just about to enter the club when I felt a tap on my shoulder. Behind me stood a huge squat hulk of a doorman. Though he didn't look particularly aggressive, he was wide and obviously very strong.

"Hey you….Yes you, you can't go in," he shouted at me, although he was just standing right next to me. I consider myself to be fairly vertically challenged, but next to him I felt quite tall.

"Would you please tell me why I'm not allowed in?" I said in my most gentle Persian English. His reply was that I was not properly dressed for the club and that consequently he couldn't let me in. There were many people in the queue, and I found the refusal very embarrassing. Naturally I looked at the other guys in the queue and compared their clothes with what I was wearing. To be frank and without being boastful, none of them was as smartly dressed as I was, but they all got in without any hassle.

I have to admit that most of the guys in the queue had jackets on but since I used to work there before, I knew that after getting in most of them would take their jackets off. That's why I wasn't wearing my jacket in the first place. As a naive and inexperienced teenager, I at first thought the doorman's refusal to let me in was genuine and that he was just doing his job.

My bedsit wasn't far away so I quickly went home and put on a formal black leather jacket. Surely they'll let me in now, I thought.

Just as I joined the queue again, the same doorman approached me. "Haven't you been told? You can't come in unless you are smartly dressed?" "I am smartly dressed and I'm now wearing a jacket." I replied with a lump of angry frustration in my throat.

"You're wearing a leather jacket and not wearing a tie, so I still can't let you in" He replied. Did I get the message! No, surprisingly I didn't. Should have I got the message? Yes, I probably should but I still thought he was just doing his job and that I should be wearing a tie.

Home again I went! I replaced the black leather jacket with a white dinner jacket (Yes, as a student, I had a dinner jacket as well!) and a black velvet bow tie. I also replaced the shoes I was wearing with a very shiny pair of black patent ones. They were so shiny that I could see my face in them. I returned to the club, this time with my chin up, knowing that I was smart enough to even meet the Queen at Buckingham Palace.

The doorman looked me up and down. "It's you again Mr Humphrey Bogart. Why don't you get it boy? I told you that you are not allowed in". The message really was loud and clear. He wasn't going to let me in. But I still didn't get it! I was only 20 and very naive.

There was a gentler looking man of some authority, standing among the doormen, whom I later discovered to be the new manager. I stupidly ignored the doorman and went towards the manager. I explained the situation and also told him that I used to work there for his predecessor. He studied me from head to toe and seemingly felt sorry for me. He asked the doorman the reason he had refused me entry. "He's a **Trouble Maker**" he replied. The manager, who I think had worked out what had gone on, smiled and asked the cocky bouncer to let me in.

I went into the club keeping my triumphant smile to myself. As soon as I got through the door I took off my bow tie, undid two or three buttons of my shirt, and put the enormous fashionable collar of my shirt out over my jacket. John Travolta was then ready to boogie the night away!

I now had a new tactic to attract the opposite sex. I had decided to make myself look either unavailable or hard to get. The tactic appeared to work. I gave a girl, that I found attractive, just one quick look and turned away. However from the corner of my eye I counted the guys who approached her and whom she rejected. I knew for sure that she was interested in me because every time after each refusal her faced turned towards me. After a while our eyes met and she gave me a smile.

She accepted my invitation to dance without any hesitation. One dance became two and two became three and so on. I was just planning my next move when I became aware of a hostile gaze boring into me. The vicious bouncer was standing not far from us, giving us both the look of death.

We finished dancing and she joined her friends for a short break. I was hungry so I went to get myself a portion of chicken & chips in a basket. As I was approaching the food counter, where Barbara and I used to serve food, someone tapped me on the shoulder. It was the doorman again. Pointing at the quiet side of the counter, he asked me if he could have a word with me. I genuinely thought that he was going to apologise and explain why he was being awkward.

"You are a c…" he said in a low voice.

I had never heard the "C" word before in my life and genuinely had no idea what it meant. Innocently I replied I'm not a c…., I'm a Persian" As you can imagine he assumed I was being a total smart arse ….

"You are a f…ing bastard" he whispered. This time I did know what he was saying, so consequently I returned his sentence back to him word for word. He raised his closed fist toward my face shouting so that his colleagues would hear "You are telling me that I'm a f…ing bastard?"

His fist landed squarely on my mouth and I felt immediate pain, as several front teeth shattered and my mouth filled with blood and fragments of tooth. I couldn't even block him. Instinctively I lashed out with my foot aiming for his crotch, but I was immediately surrounded by about nine other bouncers.

Within moments I was lying flat on the floor drenched in, mainly my own blood. The sight of ten bouncers standing above me, swearing and kicking me is an image that has lived with me ever since. Looking back on this now, I realise that the entire incident was pure racism. I hadn't thought that such behaviour could take place in the West. This was in the 1970s before race equality legislation. Such a thing is much less likely to happen today because of the legislation and because attitudes have changed so much over the intervening years. That's not to say that it doesn't still happen!

Among the group of hostile faces I noticed the manager of the club. He told me that he should have listened to his doorman and that I was indeed a Trouble Maker.

Like a carcass being thrown away, I was picked up from the floor and chucked out of the club through the back gate. I felt outraged and bitter and wanted to make a formal complaint against the doorman, but didn't know how to go about it. So although it was very late at night I gave Chani a call.

Chani kindly agreed to meet me at the local police station. The policeman who prepared the report asked if the bouncer was a short guy. My answer didn't surprise him at all because his reply was "I thought so." From talking to me, the officer soon realised that there would be no witnesses to back up my story. However Chani & I, accompanied by two police officers, went back to the club. All the bouncers, including the manager, informed the officers that they'd witnessed me swearing and kicking their colleague first and consequently they'd needed to control and restrain me.

The police informed me that this particular doorman was not only a professional boxer, he was allegedly an active member of the National Front. He'd harmed other people previously, but none of his poor victims, just like myself, had any witnesses, so they weren't able to prosecute.

The police advised that under the circumstances it would be unwise and probably futile for me to try to press charges against the doorman and his colleagues, and at that time I had no other choice but to listen to their advice.

Subsequently I experienced a great deal of excruciating pain and problems with my gums. After undergoing a number of dental surgeries during the years that followed, I now feel that I should have taken legal action against the doorman or at least against the club. Surely, even if I was making trouble, ten bouncers could easily throw a young lad out of the club without causing such significant injuries.

I had recurring nightmares about this incident, and although it was completely out of character and I knew that it wasn't healthy for me to dwell on this matter forever, the idea of confronting the doorman again took hold in my mind.

One of Britain's famous Karate champions was running a self-defence course in a nearby club, so I became a member and attended as many classes as possible; almost religiously for nearly a year. So Mr Jackie Chan Payami thought that he was ready to whisper a few Persian words of wisdom in the doorman's ear. One evening whilst socialising with a few fellow black belt students, I told them about the incident and that I intended to go back to the club and confront him. They were touched and angered by my story and realised that I'd been both physically and emotionally scarred by the incident. They all knew me as a gentle, friendly person and not someone who looks for a trouble, so to my surprise they offered their assistance.

I accepted their kind offer on condition that they must avoid fighting unless absolutely necessary, and I meant it. In addition they agree to leave the doorman, who caused the trouble, to me and would only stop the other bouncers from interfering. My idea was that I would whisper a few provocative words in the doorman's ear, to provoke him into landing the first blow. This time the so called "Trouble Maker" would be ready, and would block the bouncer's punch, giving him the benefit of my Karate lessons. This time my black belt friends would be by my side, to witness the bouncer's first move and any intention to cause serious injury.

There were a few heavily built doormen outside the club, but the doorman who had attacked me wasn't there. Mr Jackie Chan Payami and his five black belt friends got into the club without any hassle, wearing only smart casual clothes. I looked everywhere for my doorman, but he was nowhere to be seen. I asked one of the barmen who I recognised, the whereabouts of the doorman. He told me that this guy had been responsible for a bloody fight in the club and had been jailed, and given quite a long prison sentence.

Much as I might have relished my revenge, I was secretly relieved. Justice was certainly done and I felt very good about him being locked up in prison, because what he did to me both physically and emotionally was much worse than what the dogs did to my poor friend Freydoon; they had forced him out of the country!

My karate team friends and I had nothing else to do except enjoy ourselves, which we did.

There was also a funny side to this story, which took place one St. Patrick's day at another London Club. For years this has been the source of much laughter amongst my good friends Amir and Ali A, which relate to the crowns I needed to replace my missing teeth. On this certain night, we were all dancing happily with three girls that we'd met in the club, and during one of the slow dances my partner indicated that she wanted to kiss me. Needless to say I obliged. We had just started kissing when to my horror (and surely to my partner's disgust) one of my crowns dropped out! I recall the song for the slow dance was "If You Leave Me Now" by Chicago! The next song, if you can believe it was "All By Myself"! Talk about rubbing salt in the wound.

I looked around at my friends hoping for some sympathy, only to find them doubled up with laughter, clutching their bellies and gasping for air.

Baghali polo ba mahicheh

(Broad beans & dill rice with lamb shank)

For 6 people

500g Basmati rice

5 tbsps. salt (for soaking/parboiling the rice)

150ml pure vegetable oil & a knob of butter

A pinch of high quality Iranian saffron strands

3 tbsps. dried dill

800g frozen broad beans

6 lamb shanks

1 large onion, peeled and finely chopped

Ground turmeric, cinnamon & cumin - 2 tsps. each.

2 tbsps. tomato paste

2 bay leaves

6 cloves of garlic - skinned and cut into thick slices

Pure vegetable oil for frying

Salt & pepper for seasoning

1. Cook the frozen broad beans for 5 minutes in lightly salted water. Drain and peel the beans. Gently split into halves & set them aside.

2. In a saucepan large enough to cook all the shanks, sweat the chopped onion in little oil for a couple of minutes until translucent. Score the lamb shanks deeply and plug the holes with garlic slices, then seal them and brown lightly in the saucepan. Top up with boiling water ensuring that the liquid covers the shanks by about 2cm. Bring the mixture to the boil and skim off the resultant foam from the surface. Add the bay leaves, tomato paste and stir in spices, then reduce the heat. Season to taste and simmer slowly for about 2 ½ hours. Check occasionally that enough liquid remains to make a good gravy. If necessary add a little more boiling water.

3. In the meantime prepare the plain rice, following steps 1 - 5 for *Chelow* with *Tahdig* (Chpt.1)

4. Set aside a few dessertspoons of plain parboiled rice (to make the saffron garnish). Scatter a thin layer of rice over the *Tahdig*, sprinkle over a few pinches of dill and spread over a handful of the broad bean halves. Mix both layers lightly with a fork and continue the same layering process, shaping the rice into a pyramid.

5. Follow steps 7-9 for *Chelow* with *Tahdig* (Chpt.1)

6. Serve this delicious and textured mixed rice with a garnish of saffron rice on individual serving plates, alongside the tender and moist lamb shanks and crispy *Tahdig* of your choice. (My guests love to have this dish particularly with *Must-o-kheeyar* & also *Torshi-eh Liteh* as side dishes.

Hint: Scattering a pinch of finely chopped garlic on each layer, gives this dish another dimension.

Baghali polo ba mahicheh

(Broad beans & dill rice with lamb shank)

My local disco back in the 70's

This venue, which was also used for the filming of the

crime comedy Snatch (Brad Pit), was demolished in 2015.

CHAPTER 8

Spoon Beating & the Persian Festival of Fire

After passing my A' levels, I said goodbye to Chani and my romantic attic bedsit. I briefly lived with a family near my university, before renting a sunny and spacious flat in a large converted Victorian house.

At that time, one of my cousins in Iran was a prosperous and well respected Engineer (*Mohandess*). He and a few associates had their own Civil & Structural Engineering consultancy firm, and I thought that if I were to get a degree in this field, he might take me on as a graduate engineer. I therefore decided to study Civil Engineering, as I felt certain he would train me to be just as successful as he was. I also had a dream of owning a new Mercedes Benz, an ultra-modern house in the best part of the capital, and a new villa that I'd designed myself, by the lush green shores of the Caspian Sea, just as my cousin had.

Before starting at University, I returned home to celebrate the Persian New Year (*Nowruz*) with my family. The spring of 1977 turned out to be the last time that we three brothers gathered together to celebrate this occasion with our parents. As tradition goes, on the night before the New Year, like most Persians, Mum cooked us herbed rice with fried white fish (*Sabzi polo Mahi -see* Chpt.1).

Nowruz in Persian literally means 'New Day' but the word actually means New Year's Day. Iranians, whether Zoroastrian, Jewish, Christian, Muslim, Baha'is or most other faiths, celebrate *Nowruz* precisely at the time of vernal equinox (the first day of spring, on around March 21).

Nowruz, one of the most important festivals for Aryan people, has been observed annually by Persians for at least 6 millennia. However according to Ferdowsi's 'book of kings' (*Shahnameh*), the tradition takes the festival (obviously not as it stands now) as far back to 15,000 years, when King Jamshid, according to the Zoroastrian texts, apparently saved mankind from a desperately hard winter (possibly an Ice Age?) that was supposedly destined to destroy every living being. Persians also believe that it marks the first day that the universe started its motion, so we Persians even think we know the exact day when 'Big Bang' actually took place! I wonder what Professor Hawking would think about this?

On an equally dubious note, the carving of a Persian official at Persepolis makes it look as though Persians have been manufacturing the Cornetto ice cream for well over 2500 years!

One of the last celebrations of the year, of which I have many fond childhood memories, is the Persian Festival of Fire *'Chahar Shanbeh Soori'* (loosely translated as Wednesday Light or Red Wednesday). This is an old and interesting tradition, dating back to at least 1700 BCE. Although the wording refers to Wednesday, the festival actually takes place on the last Tuesday of the Persian year. This is the only time I ever recall seeing camels in the capital city. A special type of dried bush weed, brought from afar, used to be delivered to the streets by camels. People would then buy the weed and set up small bonfires in open spaces. Both young and old would then begin joyfully leaping over one fire after another with songs and gestures of merriment.

I clearly recall, whilst leaping over these fires myself, singing along with others, shouting *"Zardieh man az tow"* - *"sorkhieh tow az man"*, meaning: "I will give you my yellow colour", yellow being the sign of sickness, followed by "You give me your fiery red colour", red being the sign of wellbeing.

Before the arrival of a New Year, it's customary to put behind us all the misfortunes of the previous year. So after the bonfire ritual, and having had our evening meal, all the youngsters, and even some adults, would leave their homes for spoon beating *'Ghashowgh-zani'*. Whilst we knocked on neighbours' doors asking for treats, pots and pans would be beaten with a spoon. The neighbour would open the door, normally with a smile, and pass on a mixture of dried nuts and fruits called *'Ajil-e-Moshkel-Gosha'*, literally meaning problem-solving nuts! Eating the nuts on this night is supposed to solve all your problems. I guess it's a bit similar to trick or treating at Halloween, which is an American concept recently adopted by the British. It's very interesting how similar traditions develop in widely differing societies.

Traditionally on this festival of fire, a hearty noodle soup called *'Asheh Reshteh'* is served for dinner. I'll share the recipe for this very nourishing soup with you at the end of this chapter, in the hope that you will make it to share with all your friends and family, on a cold winter's night. It will warm not only your tummies, but your hearts as well.

Before the New Year, housewives had days, if not weeks, of preparatory work to do. This included top to bottom spring cleaning of the house (*'Khaaneh Takaani'* - House shaking!), endless shopping, and cooking of snacks and refreshments that would be required over the next two weeks of the festivities. On that last *Nowruz* in 1977, my exhausted mother found time to join her three children and her husband at our New Year's table *'Mee-zeh Haftseen'*. The table is set in a particularly traditional manner, before the exact change of the season from winter to spring (*Tah-willeh-Sal)*.

The radio counted down the seconds, joyfully announcing the start of the New Year and we all got up to kiss, hug and to wish each other a Happy New Year (s*aleh no Mubarak*). On our large, Italian-made dining room table, covered with a brand new tablecloth, which had been bought especially for the occasion, amongst other delicious treats, we had the traditional *'Haftseen'* which were beautifully arranged by us all. *'Haft'* is the Persian word for the number seven and *'Seen'* is for the letter S, so *'Haftseen'* table means a table of seven items that start with the letter S.

Unfortunately the history of *'Haftseen'* isn't clear, but what we do know is that number seven has always been significant among Aryan people. In ancient times each of the items corresponded to one of the seven creations and the seven holy immortals protecting them.

Some believe that during the time of Achaemenes (the supposed founder of the first Persian Dynasty) it was known as *'Haft-Chin'*, therefore seven items beginning with 'Ch'. Others claim that in the Sassanid era (the last period of the Persian Empire) it was known as *'Haft-Shin'*, so seven items beginning with 'Sh' which included *'Sharaab'* (wine) possibly Shiraz! However after the Arab invasion, wine was forbidden and it had to be replaced with vinegar, which in Persian is *'Serkeh"*. So somehow seven 'Sh's' changed to seven 'S's' and by doing so it was possible to preserve the ancient Zoroastrian culture and tradition in Islamic Iran.

The seven items that start with the letter 'S' in Farsi (Persian) and generally used today are:

1 - *Seeb* (Apple) - Symbolizing beauty and health.

2 - *Sabzeh* (Greens) - Wheat, lentil or barley is allowed to germinate in a flat dish for ten days or so before *Nowruz*. The green shoots are then tied up and decorated with coloured ribbons round the dish. Representing new spring growth.

3 - *Seer* (Garlic) - Symbolizing medicine, to get better or to ward off bad omens.

4 - *Sekkeh* (coins, normally gold coins) - Symbolizing wealth and prosperity.

5 - *Serkeh* (vinegar) - Symbolizing age.

6 - *Senjed* (the dried edible fruit of the Oleaster Tree) - Symbolizing love.

7 - *Somagh* (sumac berries) - Representing the colour of sunrise.

Other items that are also sometimes used with or instead of the above mentioned items are: *Sonbol* (Hyacinth) - Representing spring and *Samanoo* (A sweet pudding of germinated wheat) - Representing the reward of patience.

Almost all the '*Haftseen*' tables I have seen in my life have consisted of the following essential elements as well: A glass bowl with a few goldfish - representing life, a shiny mirror - symbolizing cleanness and honesty, a few candles - representing enlightenment and happiness, decorated cooked eggs - representing fertility, a holy book - representing faith or even the 'book of Kings' by Ferdowsi - representing Iranian identity, values and spirits.

Most people in Iran have at least a two week holiday for this festive season. The first few days are usually spent visiting the elders of the family, then the rest of the family and finally visiting friends, all in the form of reciprocated brief house visits.

On one of the coffee tables next to our designer Italian sofas and armchairs (Iranians love finely built Italian furniture), there were many goodies, enough to feed an army. As per the saying attributed to Napoleon and Frederick the Great "An army marches on its stomach", so indeed mum was well prepared to welcome any guests and also to pass on goodies to the spoon beaters during the festival of fire. On the other coffee table there was an extremely large bowl, full of exotic seasonal Persian fruits.

The Persian fruit bowls contained gigantic, very tasty, very juicy and highly aromatic, fresh ripe fruits and we would also add a few baby cucumbers to the bowl to complete the art work. I'm talking about plum-sized cherries, peach-sized plums and apricots, pomegranate-sized peaches, melon-sized pomegranates etc. I think you get the picture!

After we'd wished each other a Happy New Year, my dad, who wore his new suit and tie, as if he was going to an official meeting, briefly left the table to fetch our New Year's presents. He returned with a handful of crisp new bank notes, then slowly and dramatically, one by one, placed an entire set of them in front of each of us. We also received a few 18 carat Pahlavi gold coins. Neither my brothers nor I spent the money and, from a sentimental point of view, we kept our presents in a safe place, as if we somehow knew that this *Nowruz* would be our very last *together*. Nowadays, the smell of new books reminds me of the smell of those bank notes.

In the afternoon of New Year's Day, we all went to wish a Happy *Nowruz* to our most senior family member. My maternal granddad had lots of other visitors, including my uncle and his wife, who shared the house with him. They did all the '*mehman-navazee*', meaning looking after the guests in the Persian way, and so we and other guests were offered fruits, sweets and endless goodies.

This endless visiting of families and friends, sightseeing, eating and snacking goes on for 12 days. On the 13th day, as if not enough socialising has taken place, most Iranians leave their houses and head to the woods or mountains, along streams and riversides, to picnic with joy and laughter, as this is thought to clean one's mind from all evil thoughts. So it's considered a bad omen to stay behind indoors. These riversides, parks and fields are packed with people of all ages, celebrating Nature's Day (*Seezdah Bedar*). Seezdah means '13' and Bedar means 'to get rid of', so getting rid of 13!

At the same time cities and villages are all turned into ghost towns. A fantastic opportunity for the burglars one could say! However I can't remember a single burglary happening on this day, maybe because burglars believe it's a bad omen to be indoors as well!

When visiting the most senior member's home, every family would tell the others when, during the next 11 days, they would be doing their entertaining (*mehman navazee*). Most allowed a morning or afternoon during the 12 days to hold an open house. We had a large family and Mum and Dad also had a large circle of friends, so my dad's diary for the festive season became full after a day or two! Our visits had to be relatively short, otherwise we wouldn't have been able to visit everyone on our list. We made a few visits both morning and afternoon nearly everyday day, except of course one morning, when we ourselves had an open house.

On the afternoon of the 12th day, we stayed at home, and whilst mum prepared lunch for our next day's outing, the rest of the family, with a sense of anticipation, gathered together all the necessary things for the picnic. The mouth-watering aroma of Mum's steamed saffron rice with fresh herbs and herbs frittata (*Sabzee polo ba kookoo*) and the steamed, wrapped wine leaves (*Dolmeh*) with their various fillings, filled the house. I'll share my mum's recipe for her frittata (*Kookoo*) and two types of '*Dolmeh*' with you at the end of this Chapter.

During the visiting period, a decision was made by a few family members and close friends, to spend the '*Seezdah-Bedar*' on the banks of the Karaj River to the west of Tehran. The crystal clear river with its terraced banks and open flat green fields scattered with blossom laden fruit trees, were embraced on both sides by lush green hills and the snow-capped Alborz Mountain. The smell of the blossoms and the fresh air of the mountainside on the north breeze (*naseemeh shomal*) will stay in my memory forever.

I don't personally recall the incident, but according to my parents, when I was five we went to the same spot to escape the early summer heat of the city. Sometime after lunch, Mum and Dad noticed that I was nowhere to be seen! They obviously panicked, looked everywhere for me, and even started asking those they came across if they'd spotted me. It seemed that I'd just vanished into thin air.

The river was deep and fast flowing, so I couldn't possibly have entered and crossed to the other side. On our side of the bank there was a road and next to it the sheer, near-vertical face of the mountain, so I couldn't possibly have walked in that direction either. Although extremely unlikely in Iran, the possibility of my being kidnapped on the road by a child molester did cross their minds.

Almost everyone on the terrace joined my parents in the search for me, for several hours! Eventually a car pulled up, and through the open window a woman asked "Has anybody here lost their son?" The family seated nearest to the road, including Mum and Dad from a distance, shouted "Yes, yes". The car door was opened and a lady with a well wrapped up 5 year old boy, with a big grinning smile, got out of the car. Apparently this lady and her family were sitting on the bank about a mile down-river, when they noticed me happily swimming and being carried downstream by the current, totally unaware of any danger. So I narrowly escaped drowning and was very lucky to be spotted and rescued by this family.

On day 13, I awoke before dawn, full of excitement. We covered the roof rack of our Hillman Hunter with a large folded rug and packed its boot with all the things for our picnic, including the aluminium saucepans containing mum's delicious pre-prepared foods, a heated metal container (*samovar*), charcoal, both dry and fresh fruits, a backgammon board, a chess board, cards, a football, volleyball, ropes for making a swing and for a skipping game (*Tanaab – Bazee*), and in a safe place we put our sprouting greens, (*sabzeh*) from our *Haftseen* Table.

It took us about two hours or so from Tehran to reach our destination. When we arrived we spread out our rug on a flat surface, got the samovar going and lit the charcoal to heat up our food. According to tradition, people would also play practical jokes on each other and tell white lies (called *Do-ro-gheh-Seezdah,* the lie for the thirteenth). This is very similar to April fool's Day. It's believed to be the oldest prank-tradition in the world still thriving today, which has led many to believe that the origins of April fool's day are derived from this custom, and has been celebrated by Persians as far back as 536 BC.

The knotting of long blades of grass by unmarried girls, in the hope of finding a husband within the coming year, is also one of the customs that I recall seeing that day. Whilst knotting together the blades of grass, the wishful girls would chant "*Seezdah Bedar-Saleh degar-khune-ye showhar*". This rhyme literally means, "Next *Seezdah Bedar*, at my husband's home". It's said that when the blades of grass grow further, the knot eventually opens and their wishes would come true.

After stuffing ourselves with all the delicious food and consuming an immense number of Persian desserts, pastries, confectioneries, cakes, dried fruits and pistachios, interspersed with sips of hot, freshly brewed black or green Persian tea, we eventually ended our Persian feast by discarding our barley shoots (*Sabzeh*) into the river. The *sabzeh* are supposed to have collected all the sickness, pain and bad luck of the past year. Touching someone else's *sabzeh* on this thirteenth day or bringing it back home, therefore, is considered to be a bad omen and may invite other peoples' pain and hardship onto oneself. By throwing the *sabzeh* into running water, lethargy, exhaustion and weariness are believed to be washed away.

I remember that day, which turned out to be our very last together, as a happy and joyful occasion. Although whilst living in Europe, I have experienced a few *Seezdah bedar'*, they have never felt the same as those golden days back in Persia. Similarly, I'm sure that a European spending Christmas Day in a country half way across the world, wouldn't feel quite the same either. Having said that, I do remember being fascinated by the sight of beautifully lit and decorated, real snow covered Christmas trees in the Armenian neighbourhood near to us in Tehran. As far as I can recall, we always had a white Christmas in Tehran.

Once the festivities were over, my brothers and I left our tearful mother and father behind the closed departure gates of Mehrabad Airport and flew to three different parts of the globe. By this time Iradj and Touradj (TJ) had decided that they would never return to live in Persia again, and instead Austria and the USA respectively would be their new homes. My intention, however, wasn't the same.

Our latest Nowruz / Haftseen Table in London

Ash-eh Reshteh

(Iranian hearty winter noodle soup)

For 6-8 people

Chickpeas, kidney beans, green lentils & butter beans (120g of each)

Fresh parsley, chives, coriander, spring onion (1/2 bunch of each-finely chopped)

8 pieces of frozen spinach leaf lumps or two good handfuls of fresh spinach

2 tbsp. olive oil and 3 knobs of butter

1tbsp. dried mint.

2 large onions - finely diced

4 cloves of garlic - finely chopped

Salt & pepper for seasoning

1 tsp. of turmeric

200g of Iranian noodles *(Reshteh)* - broken up into 3cm strands (Fettuccine or Linguine are a good substitute)

3 tbsp. corn flour

For garnishing - 6-8 tbsp. of plain yogurt or preferably *Kashk* (a whey like dairy product), 2 tbsp. olive oil, 1tbsp. dried mint & crispy chopped fried onion (1 medium size would do).

1. Soak the chickpeas, red kidney and butter beans for 10 hours, changing the water a few times before final draining.

2. Sauté onion and garlic in a large pot until translucent.

3. Add chickpeas, the beans, turmeric and Sauté for a few minutes.

4. Add 2 litres of warm water and seasoning. Cover and cook on medium heat for 1 hour. Stirring from time to time.

5. Add lentils, herbs and ½ litre of warm water. Cover and cook on medium heat for 30 minutes. Stirring from time to time.

6. Break the noodle *(Reshteh)* strands into thirds. Add the noodles and spinach to the pot and continue cooking on low heat, stirring occasionally for a further 30 minutes.

7. Mix flour in 30 ml of cold water till no lumps. Stir well into the pot and carry on simmering on low.

8. After 15 minutes give the mixture a stir and check the seasoning. If necessary add more hot water to make sure you have adequate liquor for your servings. Simmer for further 15 minutes on low heat.

For Garnishing

Fry sliced onion till golden brown and caramelised. Stir in dry mint and fry for further minute or so till the mixture is crispy.

Serve in individual serving bowls. To the centre of each bowl add a dollop of *Kashk* or yoghurt and garnish with the fried onion and mint and a drizzle of olive oil.

Asheh Reshteh (Iranian hearty noodle soup)

Kookoo Sabzee

(Herb frittata)

For 6 people -as a mezze

6 large free-range eggs

150g fresh flat parsley

150g fresh coriander

150g spring onion

Fresh dill & chives. 60g of each

100g Californian walnuts, crushed coarsely

3 tbsps. dried barberries (optional)

2 tbsp. strained yogurt (Greek or Turkish)

2 tsp. bicarbonate of soda

1 tbsp. plain flour

½ tsp. ground black pepper

1 tbsp. crushed sea salt

3 tbsps. olive oil

2 knobs of butter

1. Preheat the oven to Gas Mark 4/180ºC /fan 160ºC.

2. Clean & wash all the herbs, discarding any discoloured or woody bits. Then either finely chop them all or whizz in a food processor. Depending on the size of your food processor, you may need to do this in batches.

3. In a large frying pan, fry the herbs in olive oil for a couple of minutes. If you are using a food processor, use a spatula to get all the combined and finely chopped herbs out. Add walnuts, butter, stir in the turmeric and cook on a medium heat for a further five minutes. Set aside for a further 5 minutes or so to cool down.

4. Whilst the herb mixture is cooling, in a large bowl whisk the eggs, yogurt, bicarbonate of soda, salt and pepper until all the ingredients are mixed well.

5. Add the herbs, a couple of spoonful at a time, to the egg mixture and mix in well. If you wish to use barberries add them to the mixture now and give the mixture another good stir.

6. Line a large Pyrex or ovenproof dish (preferably rectangular in shape about 3cm or so deep) with baking paper and use a spatula to help pour the mixture in. Flatten the surface of the mixture and bake in the middle of the oven for 25 - 30 minutes till cooked. In my opinion *kookoo* is better served lukewarm or cold. So I would allow it to cool before cutting into squares. Enjoy with flat bread and a side dish like *Must-o- Kheeyar* or *Must-o-Mooseer* as a mezze or with Sabzee polo as a main dish with one of the above.

Kookoo Sabzee **(Herb frittata)**

Dolmeh-ye Bargh-eh-Mo

(Stuffed blanched vine leaves)

For 6-8 people as an appetizer

A pack or jar of blanched vine leaves (obtainable from Turkish food stores) Well rinsed and drained

300g minced lamb

120g of rice, soaked and then drained

100g of yellow split peas, soaked/drained

Fresh parsley and coriander (a large bunch each) cleaned, washed and finely chopped

A good handful of mixed chopped fresh dill, tarragon and mint leaves.

6 tbsps. of virgin olive oil and 2 knobs of butter

1 medium sized onion, peeled and finely chopped

4 large cloves of garlic, peeled and thinly sliced

1 tsp. of lime juice 1 tbsp. of tomato puree

Salt & ground black pepper

1 tsp. each of turmeric & cinnamon

Salt/pepper for seasoning

A pinch of high quality Iranian Saffron strands

Note: For my vegetarian friends, I leave the meat out, adding 120g of pine kernels and doubling the quantity of rice.

1. Prepare 2 tbsps. of Saffron solution in a small cup as per recipe for Chelow (Chpt.1)

2. Sauté the split peas in little oil for two minutes. Cover with fresh water, add a pinch of salt and bring to the boil. Skim off the white foam from the surface and simmer on low heat for about 15 minutes. Stir in the rice, bring to the boil and then simmer for a further 5 minutes until the rice is parboiled and split peas are firm but cooked through. Drain off the water

3. In a large non-stick pan, sauté the chopped onion until translucent. Add the minced lamb, ½ of the sliced garlic and continue to cook, stirring frequently for about 5 minutes till the mince is nearly cooked. Add the tomato puree, rice and split peas, spices, saffron solution, 150ml of water and mix the ingredients thoroughly. Season to taste and then reduce the heat and let the mixture cook for a further 5 minutes. Toss in the herbs, a knob of butter and turn off the heat.

4. Lay a blanched vine leaf, vein side up and the pointed end facing away from you, on a chopping board. Place a tbsp. of the filling in a line across the front part of the leaf. Fold the front edge over and both sides of the leaf inwards over the filling and roll up away from you to make a cigar-shaped parcel. This does take a little practice! Carry on this process till all the ingredients are used.

5. Line the bottom of a large non- stick pan with a little oil and any unwanted leaves. This prevents the parcels from sticking to the bottom of the pot .Pack the parcels tightly layer after layer in the pan. Add the lime juice, the remaining olive oil/butter, garlic slices, seasoning and enough hot water to just cover the parcels. Put a plate on top of the parcels to hold them down and prevent them from falling apart. Bring the liquid gently to the boil, put the lid on the pan and barely simmer on the lowest heat possible. After about 45 minutes, check the parcels and if necessary add more boiling water to have enough sauce to drizzle over when serving.

Enjoy with *Must-o-Kheeyar* or *Must-o-Mooseer* with your favourite flat bread.

Wrapping Dolmeh

Dolmeh-ye Barg-eh-mo (Vine leaves dolma)

115

Dolmeh-ye Felfell

(Stuffed peppers)

For 6-8 people as an appetizer

Use the same ingredients as the recipe for stuffed vine leaves, replacing the leaves with 8 large sweet peppers.

1. Follow the recipe method 1 - 3 for the Stuffed Vine Leaves.

2. Preheat the oven to Gas Mark 5/190⁰. Cut off the crown of each pepper at about 2cm below the stem and remove the core and seeds. Pack the filling into the peppers, leaving some room for expansion. Replace the crowns and place with their open side up in a large baking dish. Pour the remaining olive oil and about 150ml water around the base of the peppers. Stir in the lime juice, remaining butter/garlic slices and season to taste. Cover the tray with foil and bake for about 45 minutes. Uncover, add more water if required to make a sauce and bake for a further 15 minutes till the peppers are soft.

3. Carefully dish up each pepper onto individual serving plates, pouring a few dessert spoons of the delicious sauce on one side of the plate with a dollop of plain yoghurt on top.

4. Enjoy with *Must-o-Kheeyar* or *Must-o-Mooseer* with your favourite flat bread.

Hint:

For a red or green sauce, in step 2, use a well-blended mix of red or green pepper, olive oil, butter, lemon juice, garlic, seasoning and stock.

Dolmeh-ye-Felfell **(Stuffed peppers)**

O Sole Mio! (one more cornetto)

CHAPTER 9

An Injection & a Revolution

The following summer, before the Islamic Revolution, I travelled to Persia alone. It was very hot that year, or maybe I noticed it more, having just experienced our wonderful British weather. I recall the average temperature at night being about 30 degrees centigrade. It was not healthy to sleep in an air-conditioned room every night, so we usually slept outside on our large, open rear balcony, in single beds with mosquito nets. Before going to bed, my father used to go into the garden to water all the plants and also spray water over the balcony, so it would be much cooler for sleeping.

One morning just before dawn, I heard an unusual noise, which resembled the sound of machinegun fire. I heard what sounded like bursts of fire coming from what I estimated to be about a mile away. After a while all was quiet and all I could hear was the sound of my dad and our neighbour on his roof, snoring. Mum and Dad didn't wake to the noise, and in the end I dismissed these sounds from my mind.

The following morning, I decided to visit the Grand Bazaar. To this day, I love the atmosphere of bazaars, especially the bazaars in Shiraz, Isfahan and also the souks in Marrakech. The Grand Bazaar in Tehran consists of over 10 square kilometres of covered stores divided into bustling, colourful and atmospheric lanes. It's an important place of commerce for all Iranians, overseas merchants and tourists alike. Most lanes specialised in a particular commodity such as gold, carpets, copper or spices, and the fascinating roar of haggling customers and merchants pervading every corner.

From our home, I took two 'Sherkateh Vahed' buses to get to the bazaar. I arrived early in the morning when business was brisk, but not yet frantic. The combined smell of fresh herbs and varieties of spices and the waft of lunch time barbecues from the kebab houses (*chelow kababees*) and even the distinctive smell of silk and woollen Persian carpets, assailed me.

However the sense of ease that I felt in these familiar surroundings was short-lived, as I noticed a bizarre sign above the entrance of one particular kebab house. The sign said "The entrance of non-Muslims is forbidden" – "*Woo rude-eh gheyreh mosalmoon ha mamnoost*". Well, I was hungry so I'm afraid I ignored the sign, went in and enjoyed a traditional mince lamb kebab with saffron rice (*Chelow Kabab-eh Koobideh*). Incredible isn't it, that in the twenty first century many people have to face and tolerate this, and many other kinds of prejudice.

On the way to the Bazaar I had to change buses at 24th of Esfand Square (*Meydoneh Bistow Chahareh Esfand*) which, after the Islamic Revolution of 1979, was renamed Revolution Square (*Meydoneh Enghelab*). At the centre of this large square before the revolution, stood a large statue of the last Shah of Iran, but on that day the statue's head was missing and two uniformed policemen were guarding the remains of the statue. I was very curious about the missing head so I walked towards the guards. Just before opening my mouth, I recalled the incident as a youth outside the clinic, and wisely decided that I should keep my curiosity to myself. As Persian wisdom has it "If something burns on your tongue, let it burn!"

On my way home I visited a few local shops. The shopkeepers didn't seem as cheerful as in the old days and I found the atmosphere everywhere very tense and wary. The headless statue of the Shah, intense atmosphere and the machinegun like noises of the morning before, all began to make me feel increasingly uneasy.

As the day went on, my sense of unease and feeling of impending trouble grew ever stronger. All my instincts were telling me that dark days lay ahead. I grew increasingly concerned about the situation and about the safety of my parents.

When my dad came home I explained what I'd seen and what my instincts were telling me. I was very emotional and felt an overwhelming sense of urgency. I told my parents that they should consider selling the house and leave Iran immediately. I told my dad they could easily buy a respectable three bedroom house in a suburb of London and live happily there without any worries.

"Those machinegun-like noises you heard were probably coming from the road works at Mehrabad Airport, otherwise I would have heard something about it in the office today. You see they sometimes have to work at night." My dad explained.

"What about the Shah's statue then?" I asked. "The missing head of the statue of the Shahan Shah (King of Kings) is more than likely due to essential repairs or accidental damage," Colonel Payami assured me.

I couldn't understand why my parents didn't feel the tension in the air, when it was so clear to me. Over the next few days I again asked them to consider leaving the country, my emotions spiralling ever higher. This time they became concerned about my health and said that living in Europe had made me imaginative (*khiyal buff*) and very sensitive (*Kheylee hass-saas*). So they took me to see our family doctor, who offered me a Vitamin B Complex injection!

Sometime after that, still with a feeling of dread, I returned to England, to my studies.

A few months later, the Islamic Revolution took place, with the persecutions and executions starting soon after this. My parents rang me to apologise for not having taken my feelings seriously. I don't know how I knew something catastrophic was about to happen, but somehow I just did.

Kabob-eh Koobideh

(Minced lamb & beef kebab)

For 6 people

600g minced lamb

600g minced beef

1 large onion

½ tsp. bicarbonate of soda

2 tsp. salt

1½ tsp.ground black pepper

1 tsp. paprika

100ml liquid saffron

Sumac for garnishing & 6 tomatoes

For grilling:

Use 12, 2cm wide metal skewers

Optional: tbsp. each- of olive oil, melted butter and saffron liquid for basting.

For the Iranian fluffy rice:

Ingredients and preparation as per *Chelow* with *Tahdig* (see Chpt.1)

1. Finely grate the onion or place in a blender, and discard the juice using a strainer.

2. In a large bowl, mix together all of the ingredients. Knead the mixture well with your fingers for at least five minutes till it resembles a sticky paste.

3. Place the mixture in a smaller bowl, cover and refrigerate for at least 3 hours.

4. When the rice is cooked (see Chap. 1) and the charcoal ready, pick up a good handful, about 100 gram, of the mixture and make it into a pear shape. Wet your hand and place the thicker end against a skewer at about 3 inches from the base and then start spreading and sticking the meat securely along the length of the skewer towards the tip by opening and closing your fingers. Make several indentations by pressing the meat between your thumb and index finger.

You need to leave 3 inches at the bottom and 2 inches at the tip of the skewer and have a thickness of meat of about ½ inch all around the skewer.

5. Grilling should start when charcoals are mostly covered in ash and grey in colour. Turn the skewers frequently for about 5 minutes each side so that the meat is cooked through evenly. I like brushing the kebabs during grilling with a mixture of olive oil, melted butter and saffron liquid.

6. Serve with Iranian fluffy saffron rice (Chelow-Chap. 1), a good pinch of sumac, a knob of butter and some grilled tomatoes. *Salad-eh Shirazi* and/or *must-o- kheeyar* (Chap1.) would go nicely with this traditional and most popular Persian dish.

kebabs to have with Persian rice (*Chelow*)

Chelow Kabab-eh Koobideh (mince lamb kebab with Persian rice)

With them the Seed of Wisdom

Did I sow,

And with my own hand

Labour'd it to grow:

And this was all the

Harvest that I reap'd—

"I came like Water, and like Wind I go."

Rubaiyat of Omar Khayyam

(Translated by: Edward Fitzgerald)

CHAPTER 10

Pierre Cardin Suit & the Curved Daggers

Soon after having my teeth repaired, I was introduced to an intelligent and attractive Irish girl named Fiona. Fiona was a student at my college and was generally an easy going girl, but like many couples we had our ups and downs. Two of those down periods, which have become tattooed on my mind are worthy of sharing. The first took place in the southern Spanish resort of Salou.

Before Fiona's *'hull-ghiri'* (act of spoiling fun), we, along with Amir and his girlfriend, were enjoying a seafood dinner in one of the resort's restaurants. I love the food in Spain, especially the dish we had that night; pasta with mussels, squid and prawns. I've made it myself many times at home, with a few modifications, and 'Mike's Seafood dish' has been very popular with our dinner guests ever since.

We were supposed to spend the next day visiting a monastery at Montserrat in the nearby mountains. However during the meal, Fiona suddenly announced that she wouldn't be joining us. She'd decided to spend the day with some friends, who were staying in Barcelona. This was going to spoil all our plans, I wasn't happy and it must have shown. Everyone at the table grew very quiet. After a few minutes, I broke the silence and although I don't recall what I said, it must have been something sarcastic and hurtful, because Fiona uncharacteristically threw the contents of her wine glass over me and then without saying a word, left the table and went straight to bed.

The following morning, Fiona got up very early, dressed and left the room. A short while afterwards I followed. Breakfast wasn't being served yet, so I went and sat with her by the swimming pool, obviously facing away from each other.

The pleasant early morning heat of the sun and the singing of the birds made me drowsy, and for a while I snoozed. I was quickly woken by Fiona, who out of the blue asked me to have a look at the swimming pool. I wasn't in the mood to make up with her, so I pretended to be asleep. "Mehrdad please... Please have a look. There looks like a body at the bottom of the pool". She was right, indeed there was a body lying flat at the bottom of the deep end!

Without hesitation, still wearing my clothes, I jumped straight in and with some difficulty managed to bring the body of an elderly man to the surface. Without considering the possibility of a head injury, the hotel staff helped pull the man out of the water, laid him by the side of the pool and then just stood there staring down at him. No one administered first aid. I think they all thought they were dealing with someone who was already dead. To be honest I did too. He wasn't breathing, his water filled stomach bulged upward up like a balloon and his entire face, especially his lips, were a purplish blue.

The man looked well over 65, but he appeared to be very fit. Bizarrely, I imagined him to be my own father, so although he looked dead, I felt I couldn't just stand there like the others doing nothing. I removed his dentures and listened for signs of breathing, but I couldn't hear a thing.

I'd discovered him below the diving board, so the possibility of a blow to his head or neck did cross my mind, and I knew that I would need to be extra careful. I worked on him for quite some time, giving probably quite amateurish mouth to mouth resuscitation and pumping his chest. But this wasn't working, so I decided to push his stomach in forcefully. Suddenly water gushed out of his mouth, like turning on a fireman's hose and his stomach deflated slightly, but still there was no sign of life.

Although I heard one of the English holidaymakers saying "that's enough", I didn't give up and continued with my sequence of mouth to mouth, and pressing on his stomach. Suddenly a further surge of water poured out of the poor man's mouth, and then miraculously he began to breathe! His purple colour began to change and I heard a loud round of applause. I placed the man in the recovery position, but surprisingly there were still no signs of any emergency services. An ambulance did eventually turn up and the poor man was taken to hospital for further treatment.

What a morning! There was me in a rather foul mood, handling a stranger's false teeth and giving mouth to mouth resuscitation to an elderly man, and at the end of it all I felt slightly sick. My empty stomach certainly didn't make me feel any better.

I later discovered that the person I'd rescued was a very fit Belgian gentleman. It seems that whilst diving into the pool, he'd knocked his head against the corner of the diving board and entered the water in an unconscious state.

Thanks to the Almighty, surprisingly, even after not breathing for such a long time, he didn't suffer any brain damage. He returned to the hotel toward the end of our week's holiday and sincerely thanked me for saving his life. He then offered me quite a lot of cash. After I refused his kind and generous gesture he offered me a drink, which I accepted just to make him happy. I didn't let on that the manager of the hotel had also been supplying my friends and I with free drinks for the rest of that week, for having saved the hotel from damaging publicity. Fiona and Amir's girlfriend did drink quite a lot of pink champagne!

Immediately after this incident, Fiona apologised and made up with her so called hero. She even decided to delay seeing her other friends and we all ended up visiting the monastery as originally planned.

The second incident involving Fiona, that I still remember very clearly, took place in the flat of my friend Ali. B in London. However this time I received no apology from her, and it was quite some time later, when my English had improved significantly, that I understood why.

Ali. B was an intelligent and bright Iranian student who was also studying Civil Engineering at my polytechnic. He was from a well-known family going back to the Qajar Dynasty (1794-1925). On this occasion we were looking at his family photographs which were truly fascinating. Our attention was drawn to a particular photograph of his father, who was an Iranian ambassador, dressed in a very distinguished looking charcoal grey Pierre Cardin suit, sitting in rather lavish surroundings, among a few Arab sheiks in their traditional robes and curved daggers. Ali informed us that the Arab gentlemen in the photo, next to his well-groomed father, were the top members of the Saudi royal family.

Fiona with an incredulous note in her voice cried out "Oh, none of your rubbish then?" "Rubbish?" I replied, "What a horrible and inappropriate thing to say. Have you lost your marbles? We are talking about my friend's father here and if you don't mind, none of his family members are rubbish! I think you should apologise straight away for the disgusting things you have just said." Poor Fiona was obviously shocked at my outburst and tried to explain that what she was saying, meant that she was very impressed at hearing about Ali's father's position in the country. I didn't want to ruin the evening so I let the matter drop until we left Ali's house.

"None of your rubbish, hah? Why couldn't you say something more appropriate, in a genuine manner like 'how impressive' instead of using the word rubbish? " I questioned. "Come-on Mehrdad, we are talking about a phrase that many people use in the English language!" she replied. I was still baffled and furious and I ignored the poor girl and refused to talk to her for days, if not weeks afterwards.

Now that I understand the context it was used in, I feel quite bad about the way I reacted, and if Fiona happens to be reading this autobiography, I offer sincere apologies for my misunderstanding.

During recent trips to Greece for our summer holidays, the misuse of the English language by local traders, has been a good source of much laughter and amusement for my family and fellow holidaymakers. I share here some of the funniest menu entries I have noticed during my travels!

Soup of Moulds, Cod Paving Stone & Flaming Papers , Moulds & Snail, Wet Lamp surprise (electrifying good).

Flight with the wind of Poolard, Vet hamburger wid mashroom, Araignée de Boeuf (Tender-more or less nervous), Freed Egg Plants, Plate roasted with Poolard, Mitre with shallots (For DIY fans).

Delishez grilled Aborigine ((no comment), Moulds in garticky butter, parked with??????, Flaming papers & ?????? (Very fiery)

PS: During our last holiday to Greece, we had some Moulds, parked with ??????. It was garticky alright and there is no question about it!

Today's special

Lamp Head! & Octopus Soup (crunchy & electrifying good)

Mike's Seafood

For 6 people as an appetizer

Fresh mixed seafood – 120g per person

I use a mix of Prawns, Squid and mussels

120g of Conchiglie (small pasta shells)

3 cloves of garlic, finely diced

A handful of chopped fresh coriander/parsley mix

3 tsp. of basil pesto (or preferably make your own)

A pinch of high quality Iranian Saffron strands

Salt and ground black pepper to taste

120g of grated Mozzarella or Emmental

Virgin Olive oil & a knob of butter

Lemon or lime quarters

Green salad leaves

6 large scallop shells for serving (optional)

1. Make 100ml of saffron liquid as per Chpt.1

2. Cook the pasta in salt water for a few minutes till al dente. Drain and set aside.

3. In a non-stick frying pan, sauté the garlic in a few tbsp. of olive oil. Stir in the seafood, butter and season to taste. Fry for 3 to 4 minutes till the seafood is just cooked through. The prawns should be pink and the seafood pieces, especially the calamari, should be tender but not chewy. Stir in the basil pesto and saffron liquid. Toss in the pasta and give the mixture a stir. Spoon the mixture into the scallop shells or onto individual serving plates. Sprinkle over a little grated cheese and place under a grill till the cheese has melted.

4. Garnish with the coriander/parsley mix and serve with lemon/lime quarters and your favourite green salad. Enjoy with crunchy French bread or with slices of fresh delicious *Noon Barbary* (a type of flat Iranian bread with sesame seeds on top), available in most Turkish food stores.

Hint: To make your own Basil Pesto;

Crush and grind 2 cloves of garlic and a pinch of rock salt using a medium size pestle and mortar. Add a handful of pine nuts and a bunch of basil leaves and pound to a coarse paste. Stir in 2 tbsps.of extra virgin olive oil and 1 tbsp. of grated Parmesan. Carry on bashing and pounding to a smooth paste. Stir in a tsp. or so of water if required

Mike's Seafood

Fath-Ali Shah Qajar

(The second Shah of the Qajar dynasty- 1797-1834)

Qajar dynasty coins

These coins were given to me by grandad (Allahverdi),

50 years ago, as a Nowruz present

CHAPTER 11

The English Couple's Campervan

One day, during my last summer holiday in Iran, I noticed a Volkswagen campervan parked on open ground in front of my parents' house.

My friends and I used to play volleyball and football on that ground, and sometimes the local butcher and shopkeepers used to join in and play along with us.

When I was a child there were shops nearby selling almost everything. There was a butcher (*Ghassabee*) and a baker (*Naanvaee*). This baker made the most delicious wholemeal bread, topped with poppy seeds, called '*Sanghak*'. The bread was baked on a bed of hot shingles. There was also a general store, a hairdresser and a pharmacy.

It turned out that the campervan belonged to an English couple, and within an hour or so we soon discovered that their intention was to camp exactly opposite the house, within only thirty metres of the front doorstep. They were making quite a bit of mess and were rather spoiling our view of the Alborz Mountains. Forty years on, this area is now completely built upon, and the wonderful view we had, alas consigned to history.

My mother monitored their activities that day with some curiosity. The following morning as she was watching them washing their faces with water from a plastic container, she told me "This is not right son." "What isn't Mum?" I asked. At first I thought she wasn't happy with the mess they were making, but I soon learned that she was feeling quite uneasy, being in a comfortable air-conditioned house whilst we allowed the 'guests of our country' (as she put it) outside our house, spend their visit without running water, a toilet, or somewhere comfortable to sleep.

"Mum, you don't need to worry about them, they'll have bought the campervan specifically so they can camp anywhere they want, to avoid paying hotel or campsite tariffs." I explained. "Still I don't feel comfortable about it Mehrdad," she replied. Mum asked me to go over to the couple and invite them for dinner that evening!

I informed her that in England, law-abiding and well-integrated people like myself were being told to 'F' off and go home, and there she was not only asking me to welcome messy foreign campers, but also to invite total strangers in for dinner. But she insisted, "We must not lower ourselves to the level of a handful, misinformed fascists. Come on, they look decent enough, go and speak to them please."

The couple were delighted to accept Mum's kind offer and made their way to our house that evening. I recall the main dish of our dinner that night was a chicken casserole with carrots and prunes (*Khoresht-eh Aloo- o –havij*) with *Chelow* rice. I'll share her recipe with you at the end of this chapter.

They proved to be a very nice couple indeed and we all got on well. The evening, although a bit tiring for me as 'translator', went well and the conversation flowed quite easily. Towards the end of the evening, my parents discussed how best to show 'the guests of our country' real Persian hospitality, and asked me to offer them the rear garden to set up their tent, so they could use our bathroom. They were amazed at my parent's generosity and without hesitation gratefully accepted! They set up their tent in our beautiful rear garden and happily spent a few days there, before heading off on their travels. Needless to say Mum wouldn't allow them to eat a takeaway, so we shared our dinner with them every night! In addition, on the last day of their stay, we shared even our lunch with them. They loved Mum's roasted aubergine dish, baked in a garlicky tomato sauce (*Mirza Ghasemi*- see Chap1), which we had with fresh, hot *Noon Barbari* (Barbari naan).

My short summer holiday visit was soon over and just like the previous summer, I had to leave Mum and Dad behind the closed departure gate of the Mehrabad International Airport and head off towards sunny England.

In mid-January 1979, a few Persian friends and I were sitting in the gloomy TV room of the polytechnic when the news of the Shah's sudden and unexpected departure from Iran into exile was broadcast. For many months after that we all gathered there every lunchtime to find out the latest news and happenings back home. Two weeks after the Shah's departure, in the resulting power vacuum in

Iran, Ayatollah Khomeini returned to Tehran from exile. On the 11th February, shockingly the royal regime collapsed and within seven weeks or so Iran became an Islamic Republic.

It was in that same TV room, and with the same crowd of friends that we heard the sad news of the public executions of the generals and ministers that had been loyal to the Shah, and where we heard news of the death of the Shah from cancer only a year and half after his exile.

The gloom of that TV Room was somehow a fitting background for the daunting clips of the many public executions and of the dead bodies of once well respected and well known officials . We were all increasingly despondent and worried for our families and friends in Iran. I remember that we just couldn't comprehend what was happening to our hitherto peaceful and rapidly developing country. Progress had stalled, and it seemed that Iran was now travelling back in time with consequences we couldn't even begin to imagine.

I must add here that the Iranian students, who were present in that room, didn't all share the same point of view about the revolution, some, to the amazement of my friends and I, actually found the whole thing, including the public executions, a reason for joy and celebration.

Had I not been the son of a Colonel loyal to the Shah, or had I not as a teenager, been so lucky in my encounters with the police or security forces, who knows maybe I would have welcomed a peaceful, bloodless change in the regime, but I would never have welcomed any form of violence and certainly wouldn't have celebrated the deaths of those individuals, wherever their loyalties lay.

Unfortunately such extreme reactions aren't uncommon among many of my countrymen. Neither is the adoration they can bestow on royalty or political and religious leaders. Whether such reactions stem from personal or financial reasons, or are linked to social status, or simply due to ignorance, I'm just not sure. Whilst I'm accustomed to seeing such extreme reactions, I know they will baffle people in the west.

In my youth one often saw portraits and photographs of the Shah on the walls of people's houses and in public places. These images were kissed and bowed before, by people from all levels of Iranian society. I have no doubt the Shah's hands and shoes on these images were liberally coated in his subjects' DNA as a result of their reverence! Perhaps older generations in the UK showed similar reverence to portraits of the King or later Queen Elizabeth, though never to politicians, except possibly Winston Churchill.

So it was galling for me to observe that many of these fellow citizens, who had until then idolized the figure of the Shah, transferred their loyalties chameleon-like to the Ayatollah, burning the portraits they had so recently adored and celebrating the death of one upon whom they had, a few years back, wished a long life. It felt like yesterday, during the Shah's White Revolution, that millions were gathered in the streets shouting long live the king ("*Javid Shah*").

To some of my readers I have to say that, yes I'm aware that the Shah's regime (as he himself surprisingly admitted in the last few days of his reign) had flaws and that the Pahlavi regime, like many other regimes, had ample room for improvement. Serious flaws with respect to some aspects of Human Rights and the mistreatment of many people, especially of political opponents, by some members of the secret service were among these flaws. I understand and do believe that the Shah was trying to rectify some of these issues in the latter years of his reign.

It is said that soon after hearing about the widespread demonstrations against the monarchy, the Shah asked his helicopter pilot to fly him over the capital. After seeing all the demonstrators, the Shah with tears in his eyes asked the pilot "Are all these demonstrations really against me?" "Yes I'm afraid so your Majesty" the pilot answered. However what is certain, and unfortunately what the Shah did not see, was that many of his countrymen were loyal to him and stayed perplexed and surprised by this turn of events.

Soon afterwards, the Shah made an emotional national announcement that he'd heard the voice of the nation's revolution, that he was aware of the flaws in his regime, and had been trying to rectify them. However by then it was all too late. During the preceding years, his regime had alienated some Iranians through its social and economic reforms. In addition many people could no longer tolerate the terror and distrust caused by Savak's operations and they had no one else to blame but the Shah himself. As the phrase goes "the buck stopped with the Shah, as head of state."

Savak agents were felt by many to be above the law and one never knew, whether in public places or even at private parties, if the man standing next to you was a Savaki. My father's army colleagues would imagine that my dad was an army agent (*Rowkneh Dow Officer*) and my dad would think the same way about his colleagues. The atmosphere of fear and betrayal permeated all of society and in the end, in my opinion this was a factor in the downfall of the late Mohamad Reza Shah Pahlavi in 1979. Having said all this, the most important factor was oil, and the Shah's speech to OPEC back in 1973. He expressed his intention to free Iran from unfair oil contracts that were due to end in 1979. The Carter administration's efforts in supporting Ayatollah Khomeini in France, and also in neutralising the Iranian armed forces, led to the success of the revolution. I understand that many loyal generals were planning for a military takeover, and they urged the Shah not to leave, however he didn't want any bloodshed, so opted to leave.

Putting the regime's flaws to one side, it's evident, in two of the Shah's books 'Towards Great Civilisation' and 'Mission for My Country', that he was a patriot, and had a great vision for Iran. The problem was that the nation wasn't yet ready. You can't make a toddler run a Marathon can you? He wanted too much too soon.

Many of those Iranian students who supported the 1979 revolution returned to Iran, and quite a few managed to get well paid jobs working for the new government. I even heard that one student with us in that dull TV room, became an important figure in the newly formed secret service, which according to many, continued to terrorise and mistreat people, and has proved to be worse than the old Savak.

The rest of us, who were uneasy with the regime change or believed in a secular government, found little choice but to settle abroad, far from our homeland. We had to confront the possibility of making a new beginning, far away from our emotional and cultural home and far from our families. This is a daunting prospect at any time, but even more so at such a young age and where cultural differences were so great. Iranians were not generally welcomed because of the new Iranian regime's hostility towards the west.

Soon after the revolution, the persecution and executions of religious minorities, especially the Baha'is started. The appalling treatment of the followers of the largest religious minority in the country became so savage, that it attracted the attention of the media and governments all over the world, as well as the United Nations and other international organisations.

Many members of Baha'i' Spiritual Assemblies, distinguished academics, industrialists and many ordinary Baha'is all over Iran were arrested, executed, and their homes, lands and belongings were either confiscated or destroyed. Things became so bad that the members were openly denied employment and their children expelled from schools and universities.

William Sears, author, humourist, and former TV star and also one of the most distinguished Baha'is, in 1982 wrote a very moving book about the persecution of the Baha'is called 'A Cry from the Heart'. In the book there is an impassioned account of the horrors perpetrated against innocent Baha'is. Since the first major demonstration against the Shah in January 1978 till 15 December 1981, 82 executions where the victims were burned or stoned to death were reported. In the same book we are told that within the same period, 94 Baha'i believers were reportedly imprisoned and many others reported missing. All of these figures are taken from official sources.

Because of the on-going unrest in Iran and the possible risk of being arrested, prosecuted or worse , like many innocent people, for no legitimate reason whatsoever , I felt uncomfortable to return home even just for a short visit.

Furthermore I was still eligible for my two years compulsory military service. I therefore decided to extend my student visa by undertaking a post-graduate course. I soon managed to obtain UK citizenship, visited a commissioner of oaths, as new citizens did in those days, and swore loyalty to her Majesty the Queen.

Mirza Ghasemi

A roasted aubergine dish, baked in a garlicky tomato sauce- see Chap

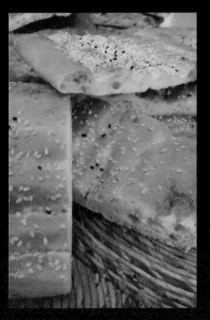

Noon Barbari (Barbari Naan)

Khoresht-eh Aloo- o –havij

(Chicken casserole with carrots and prunes)

For 6 people

12 chicken portions

6 large carrots - cut into batons

1 large onion - finely chopped

6 dried prunes (Californian) per person

1 tsp. turmeric

2 tsps. cinnamon powder

2 tbsp. tomato puree

Salt and pepper for seasoning

Olive or any other pure vegetable oil

A knob of butter

For the Iranian fluffy rice

Ingredients and preparation as per *Chelow* with *Tahdig* (see Chpt.1)

1. Discard any skin and fat from the chicken.

2. In a non-stick frying pan, sauté the chopped onion and carrots in a little oil for about three minutes. Add the spices, give the mixture a stir and transfer to a saucepan.

3. Fry the chicken portions in the same pan for a few minutes on each side until golden and then place them in the saucepan. Add the tomato puree, butter and dried prunes. Top up with hot water to a level of about 2cm above the mixture. Give the contents a stir, bring to boil and then simmer on low heat for about an hour or so until the chicken is thoroughly cooked and the carrots are soft and tender. Halfway through, check the seasoning. If necessary add more hot water and maintain a liquor cover of about 2 cm till the end of cooking.

4. Carefully empty the casserole with its thickened sauce into a deep platter or present it delicately on individual serving plates next to cooked fluffy rice serving the sauce separately.

5. Accompany with the *Chelow* and *Tahdig* (Chpt.1) & your favourite Iranian side dish/es

Khoresht-eh Aloo- o -havij

(Chicken casserole with carrots and prunes)

Chelow (Iranian fluffy rice) with ***Tahdig***

Towards the Great Civilisation

(By Mohamad Reza Shah Pahlavi)

"As the saying goes,

"You can lead a horse to water but you can't make him drink'."

CHAPTER 12

Winter Solstice & the Blood Thirsty Bats

A few months before deciding to undertake my post graduate course, Fiona told me that as part of her degree course she'd have to spend a year in Spain. Our relationship was becoming more serious, and I felt that I just couldn't bear to be apart from her for a whole year. I thought that a little Spanish sunshine and warmth would also do me some good and would cheer me up, as I'd been brooding about events back home. It certainly hadn't occurred to me that she wouldn't welcome my intention to accompany her to Granada.

In the end I did remain in London. Fiona felt that my presence in Spain would prevent her from settling in and getting to know the local people. To be honest at that time, I tended to be rather jealous, and in retrospect I can perhaps see how she felt. She was worried that I would be over-protective, preventing her from socialising and learning the language properly. A few months after she left, she actually started to miss me, and phoned to ask if I would join her, but by this time I'd started my post-graduate course, and although I still really cared for her, I wasn't going to jeopardise my newly laid plans.

At the beginning of the academic year I found myself a part-time night job, working in what I understood to be, at that time, the only twenty four hour petrol station in south London. This job suited me perfectly, because after midnight I hardly had any customers. Possibly a car or two, mainly taxis, would pull up every hour or so, but apart from that I had a lot of spare time to study. I could earn money and continue with my coursework at the same time!

I finally completed my course and realised that I needed to find a better job. One day, as I was walking around Knightsbridge, I noticed a sign requiring trainee managers, advertised in the window of an up-market shoe shop. I applied and got the job. My thinking was that it would do as temporary job, until I found work in my own field. Curiously, my future wife, Imogen (with an Archaeology degree), started work also as a trainee manager in the same shop on the very same day! With some really hard work and dedication, within a year we both became managers of our own west end shops.

That Christmas, Fiona returned home for the festive season and appeared to have missed me. However, during her subsequent short visit at Easter, it was clear that something had changed. At first I thought perhaps "out of sight out of mind" had cooled her feelings for me, but the invitation to join her for the summer seemed to prove otherwise.

I eagerly counted down the days until my trip. I was still very much in love and had stayed faithful to Fiona throughout her year of absence.

One week before I was due to fly out, I was attending a training session in retail management and for some reason, suddenly lost all of my usual cheerfulness, and felt strangely panicky. Cold sweat covered my skin and within the space of a few minutes I felt quite unwell. It was the strangest physical feeling I'd ever experienced.

The branch manager became very worried, and although he was short staffed, he sent me home to rest. I don't really know why, but when I got home, instead of going straight to bed, I called Fiona, hoping to find her in. Unfortunately she wasn't. It was the middle of the day, and I realised she would have been at lectures, but her English room-mate answered the phone, and I asked her to tell Fiona that I would be ringing later on that evening. There was a worrying silence at the end of the line, and when I questioned her, she told me something like "that won't be necessary". I asked her to explain what she meant, to which she replied" Please don't ask me any more questions" and hung up.

Had Fiona had an accident? This was the first question I asked myself, followed by a series of other worrying thoughts. To distract myself, I went to make a cup of strong Turkish coffee, but before I reached the kitchen the telephone began to ring. I ran quickly and picked it up. "Hello Mehrdad" it was Fiona. "Thank God," I said to myself. "Are you okay Fiona? You sound very shaky". "No I'm not" she replied in an unsteady voice. She then told me that she was in London and that she would like to see me straightaway, refusing to say anything else.

Was she in some sort of trouble? Had she been involved in an accident that would require her to have serious medical attention over here? Or had she, God forbid, developed a serious illness? These were questions I was asking myself, whilst driving like a maniac to her mother's flat.

Fiona opened the door and seeing her in one piece relaxed me. She hugged me and began to weep. She cried for some minutes, her cheek on my shoulder, soaking my shirt with her tears. I could hear her heart beating, fast and loud.

When she began to settle I asked her "What's this all about Fiona? Are you unwell?" "No I'm okay, well in one way, but I have to tell you something serious," she replied. She paused, and then like a volcano she let it all out. She said she'd had ample time in Spain to think about our relationship and had come to the conclusion that the relationship must end. "And you came to this conclusion after wasting a year of my time?" I commented. I told her that there must be someone else in Spain involved in this, but she assured me there wasn't. I found that difficult to believe so I repeated this, to which she replied "If there was someone else, do you think I would be here now?"

She told me that she would never have the qualities that I would expect from a partner, that she felt she couldn't meet my high expectations and that these were related to my middle-eastern heritage and disciplined upbringing. "We must end the relationship here Mehrdad," she reiterated tearfully, but with determination. Looking back I suppose I must have had a sixth sense that all was not well, and this might perhaps explain the sudden illness I'd experienced at work that day.

I tried to ease the situation, assuring her my expectations were not so very different from those felt by anyone who puts a lot into a relationship. But it was clear that she wasn't going to change her mind, and that nothing I could say or do would persuade her otherwise.

I was so disappointed and even quite angry, that I slammed the door and drove back home, just as dangerously as I had on the way over. However halfway home I calmed down a bit, changed my mind and did a U-turn. I thought, I just couldn't simply let her go just like that. I rang the bell and she opened the door without any hesitation. She was still tearful, and we hugged each other again, but I knew then she'd made up her mind and nothing was going to change that.

Fiona made me a cup of tea and again assured me there was no one else involved, which settled me. She said that she'd come all the way from Spain just for that day, to tell me about her decision face to face. At the time I thought to myself "Oh yeah, who do you think you're kidding?" but the very next day, she was indeed back in Spain and I felt I needed to thank her over the phone for her decency and respectfulness.

On the way home, being young and male, I couldn't stop myself from dwelling on the times and opportunities that I perceived myself as having lost! I was beginning to realise that women were wired differently from us poor men, and it took me a long time to really understand the reason for Fiona's decision.

I remember one particularly attractive woman who kept coming into the shop, spending hundreds of pounds on matching designer shoes and handbags, and giving me sultry looks. Every time she came in, she insisted I serve her, apparently because I knew what I was talking about and knew my stock! Being of a monogamous and faithful disposition, she received no reaction from me. Having failed to elicit a response she then changed tactics.

One day when I was adjusting the window display, a black limousine pulled up and parked on double yellow lines, right in front of the shop. A uniformed chauffer courteously opened the rear door and this rather stunning lady elegantly stepped out. It was the same woman, and yes she again asked if I would serve her. She was wearing a tight and somewhat transparent mesh dress and very high yellow stilettos. It was hilarious; I looked like Danny DeVito standing next to Jerry Hall!

Ms Mesh sat herself comfortably on a sofa in the middle of the shop facing a mirrored wall. As she tried on endless pairs of shoes it soon became apparent that she was err … doing a Sharon Stone in Basic Instinct! (Uncrossing her legs and exposing herself!) I veered somewhere between fascination and horror!

Well, I was still in love with Fiona at the time and didn't react. On her next visit to the shop, unsurprisingly she didn't ask for me, and I heard that she'd asked another member of staff if I was gay.

I must admit that after my breakup with Fiona, I did so wish that she'd return to the shop so I could disprove her suspicions!

Fiona decided to live permanently in Spain and became a teacher. We kept in touch, but only as friends, just for a few years.

In Southampton my friend Amir met Ali A, (remember the lamb's head in the saucepan!) and they forged what has become a life-long friendship. After both completing their degree courses, they returned to London to undertake post-graduate courses. A reunion with Amir and his great friend was much welcomed, and we spent many happy times together for a couple of years or so. Although recounting some of our adventures here might have amused you, unfortunately, some of them can only be revealed posthumously. As the notorious phrase goes 'what goes on in Vegas stays in Vegas', or in this case a red convertible Mercedes!

For a long time Imogen and I were just good friends, which does have the advantage of knowing each other pretty well, before things eventually advanced onto another level.

One day in July 1981, Imogen and my friend Ali.B (None of your rubbish Ali) were guests in my flat. I was making a pot of tea in the kitchen when the phone rang. My friends gently broke the news of my father's death to me. I couldn't believe that Colonel Daryoosh Payami, who was only 65, had passed away. He died of a stomach ulcer, something that with treatment using modern medicines is hardly ever fatal.

I longed to return to Iran for his funeral, but this sadly just wasn't possible. Baha'is all over the country were still being persecuted and killed, so it was far too risky for me to return home. In addition, as far as the Iranian authorities were concerned, my education was complete, and I would therefore have been forced to join the army, serving the obligatory two years of national service.

The day following my father's death, I was sitting alone in the living room, miserable, homesick and feeling hopeless. Tears ran down my cheeks. Suddenly the living room door burst open, and Colonel Daryoosh Payami, in full dress uniform with medals shining, slowly entered. He seemed in the prime of life, unlike in later years when he was thin and looked permanently anxious, as indeed he was, particularly for my mum. "My son (*Pesaram*) why are you sad and crying. I'm happy now. I'm free of any pain and the misfortune of life. So please share this happiness with me". He said these words to me gently, with a smile on his face and then disappeared. I never saw him again in this way, even in my dreams. Whether this event happened purely in my imagination or I really was visited by the spirit of my father is still a mystery to me. But it definitely happened, of that I'm certain.

My father narrowly escaped death once, many years before. I was fifteen and remember walking back home from granddad's home in the early hours of the morning with my parents, after spending an evening celebrating with family and close friends. The tree lined streets were carpeted with a thick layer of snow and because of this; it was so light that it almost felt like daytime. We were all holding hands to prevent us from slipping and sliding, talking about what a great time we'd had at granddad's, and we joked all the way home. I remember Dad's smoker's cough being much worse than usual, but we thought it was because he'd been puffing away almost throughout the fifteen minute journey. When we arrived home, we went straight to bed as dad had to go to work later that morning.

That night was a special one, because it was 'the night of Yalda' *(Shab-eh Yalda)* meaning re-birth (of the sun). It's during this time that friends and family gather together on the eve of the winter solstice (usually 21st Dec) to read poetry (especially *Hafez*), tell jokes, eat and drink until well after midnight. So we, like Persians for several thousand years before us, had been celebrating the birth of Mithra, the Persian angel of light, the triumph of light and goodness over the power of darkness.

It's said that Mithra was born out of a bright light that came from within the snow-capped Alborz Mountain. Legend has it that ancient Persians would gather in caves throughout the night to witness this miracle at dawn.

On this night it's customary to eat pomegranates, nuts, and other fruits and festive foods. So before leaving for granddad's, Mum cooked a hearty chicken stew with walnuts and pomegranates (*Khoresht-eh Fesenjoon*).

Granddad's *Shab-eh Yalda* table was always lavish. Amongst the delicious spread were pomegranates, a huge honeydew melon, watermelon, a large bowl containing nuts and dried fruits, many candles and of course a copy of '*Divan-eh-Hafiz*', one of the best works of Sufi poetry by *Hafiz-eh-Shirazi*, which can be found in most Iranian households. The red colours of the pomegranate and watermelon symbolise the glow of the sunrise and the triumph of light over darkness.

Before the revolution, and the ban on alcohol, the drinking of good Iranian wine was part of the celebration for many people. However, I've heard that the ban made many people experts in producing homemade alcoholic drinks, and many families continue to include contraband wine in their celebrations.

Before my grandfather allowed any poetry reading, jokes or storytelling to commence he said a prayer, thanking the Almighty for all the blessings we'd received over the past year, wishing continued health and prosperity for us all in the coming months. He then cut the honeydew melon and gave everyone a share.

It's an ancient myth that says the cutting and sharing of melon by the oldest member of the family symbolizes the removal of any pain and sickness from friends and family. And although he shared out melon that night, this superstition certainly didn't work for my poor father, especially in the days and weeks that followed.

It's also believed that in pre-Islamic Zoroastrian tradition, the *Shab-eh Yalda* celebration was intended to protect people from evil and dark forces during the longest night of the year. Consequently people were advised to stay awake with their loved ones throughout the night. Perhaps we should have followed this advice and stayed awake that night!

My panicked mother woke me just before dawn, only a couple of hours after we'd gone to bed. I promptly jumped out of my warm bed and saw my father lying motionless in bed, his eyes wide open. The curtains to our back garden were drawn back, so he must have opened them before lying down.

Looking out of the window, the garden and all the trees were heavily laden with snow. Even the flat vertical surfaces were white with the driven snow. The only contrast was the bright orange colour of a few remaining Sharon fruits on our persimmon trees. The sight of abundant Sharon fruits weighing down the leafless branches and their attractive colour usually warmed my heart and made me smile. I remember this scene, frozen in that moment with a clarity induced by my feeling of total panic. Somehow though, the fiery coloured fruits seemed to represent hope.

My father suddenly blinked a few times, began shaking violently, turned his head away from us, as though he couldn't see us or didn't recognise us, focused his eyes on the bare wall and froze.

Unfortunately our phone was dead; it later transpired that the heavy snow had caused a problem with the phone lines in our neighbourhood, so my mother asked me to run for help. I called on a neighbour who agreed to stay with mum, and then, although I didn't have a driving licence, I managed to start our car, intending to drive to the hospital. The snow was so deep however; that I couldn't move the car, not even an inch.

I ran as fast as I could through the deep snow for half a mile or so, till I got to the nearest roundabout where I stopped a passing army jeep and asked the driver if he could take me to the nearest clinic. It was still snowing heavily as I returned home in an ambulance, which struggled on the hill and started sliding. I remember jumping out to help the paramedic push the vehicle up the hill, all the while my heart fluttering with anxiety about my father.

They took my father, along with us to the nearest clinic. A few hours later one of his army colleagues, a Savaki colonel who my family knew well, and who was a decent and humane man (yes, there were many decent Savakis as well) arrived at the clinic. How he knew we were in the hospital with my father, still puzzles me to this day.

He knew my father hadn't joined Savak and consequently, like many other senior officers, was on a fairly low salary. As mentioned earlier, for most ranks in the Shah's army the salary was rather low but the benefits were excellent. To avoid embarrassing my mother he quietly pulled me to one side, opened his wallet and offered me a significant amount of money. "Your dad is a very decent and well respected friend and he deserves to be treated in the best hospital and not in such a basic clinic as this. Please accept this money and get your dad to Mesaghieh or Jam-eh Jam hospitals". Though I appreciated his kind offer greatly, I told him that arrangements had already been made to take my dad to Tehran's military hospital.

My father used to smoke pipe and nearly two packs of cigarettes a day, despite our family doctor on many occasions, warning him of the dangers. My mother also had endless arguments with him about this. Trying to avoid these arguments, and pretending he'd cut down, Dad used to tuck cigarettes in his socks and secretly smoke in the toilet. He was caught out by mum several times, but generally he'd get away with it. Remembering this somewhat childish behaviour still brings a smile to our faces, when we talk about the old days.

During his first month of hospitalisation, Mum and I visited if not twice, at least once a day. Throughout this time he didn't recognise us and didn't once ask for a cigarette. Sometimes he was silent, other times he talked a weird form of gibberish, again without any sign of recognition. It was terrible seeing him like this, lying silently, just staring into the distance every day. His illness, which proved to be pneumonia, back in the late sixties used to kill more people than it does today.

One evening I had a nightmare. I was surrounded by hundreds of blood thirsty bats, flying all around me. It was more terrifying than a scene from Hitchcock's film 'The Birds'. However every bat, just as it began to attack, would be hit with a ray of light and I soon found myself surrounded, absolutely unharmed, by a carpet of fallen dead bats. The morning after this unusual dream, my dad's first words to us were "Good morning you two. I could really fancy a cigarette right now". We were never more relieved to hear him say those words.

My mother was so overjoyed to have her husband back, that she gave me some money and told me "Run - run, get a packet of Winston cigarettes and come back quickly." *"Bodow Bodow yek pakat-eh Winston cigar bekhar va zood barghard."* Dad did recover fully from this illness, but the experience didn't stop him from inhaling his forty a day in the subsequent years. Our family doctor told us that his smoking habit, together with the stress associated with the revolution, caused the incurable ulcer that eventually took his life.

Shab-eh Yalda (Our winter solstice celebration in London)

My nightmare about the bats attacking

(Perfectly illustrated by my dear son Cameron)

Khoresht-eh Fesenjoon ba morgh

(Chicken Stew with walnuts and pomegranate)   For 6 people

2chicken thighs or 3drumsticks per person. Occasionally, I would use boned thigh (diced)

1 large onion - peeled and finely chopped

400g of walnuts (I prefer Californian) - finely ground

200ml of pomegranate molasses

A pinch each of turmeric & cinnamon

3 tbsps. olive or other pure vegetable oil

Salt and pepper

2 tsps. caster sugar or honey

A knob of butter

For the Iranian fluffy rice

Ingredients and preparation as per *Chelow* with *Tahdig* (see Chpt.1)

1. Add a tbsp. of oil to a frying pan, and cook the onion in until translucent and golden. Sprinkle over the spices, give the mixture a stir and transfer to a large saucepan.

2. Discard any fat from the chicken and using the same pan, fry until sealed and slightly browned. Add to the onion mixture giving it a good stir. Pour over about 450 ml of water and bring to the boil, reduce the heat and simmer for 15 minutes.

3. In a frying pan, toast the walnuts until they start to darken, ensuring they don't burn. Add these, together with the pomegranate molasses to the chicken broth at the end of the 15 minutes. Simmer further on a low heat for about 45 minutes until the sauce has thickened. Half way through cooking stir gently, add a couple tsps. sugar or honey, season to taste. Add more water if necessary. This will give you a delicious, sweet, tangy and nutty gravy of the consistency of melted chocolate.

4. Serve it hot with *Chelow with Tahdig* (Chpt.1) and a side salad dish.

Hint: Adding a knob of butter towards the end of cooking, gives the dish a lovely sheen. Don't worry about any oil on the surface of this dish. It's mainly oil from the walnuts which is good for you.

Fesenjoon can also be made with duck, rabbit or meat balls.

For my vegetarian friends, I would simply replace the chicken with vegetable stock and chickpeas.

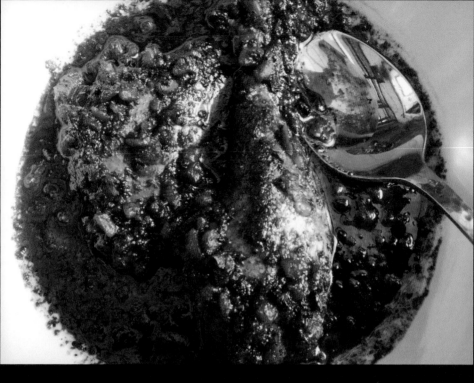

Khoresht-eh Fesenjoon ba morgh

(Chicken Stew with walnuts and pomegranate)

Chelow (Iranian fluffy rice) with *Tahdig*

Dad (on the right) in the 60's

My father's pipe & lighter

CHAPTER 13

Evin Prison & the Lamb Stew (to die for!)

Following the death of my father, the new Islamic regime didn't pay the widow's pension that my mother was entitled to. This decision was simply based on mother's faith (Baha'i). I also recall Mum telling me that they even forced her to pay back a year of my father's final salary! This money represented nearly all of my parents' life-savings. After the revolution, as part of their nationwide persecution of Baha'is, the new regime forbade the followers of this peaceful faith from undertaking any role in the public sector or armed forces. However, as far as I'm aware, this 'law' was not officially written down. This had enabled the General who'd been my father's boss to turn a blind eye, and allowed my father to carry on working for the gendarmerie wing of the armed forces for a year or so after the revolution began.

Their house in Tehran soon became too big and difficult for Mum to manage. In addition to the physical strain of looking after such a big house, thanks to the new regime, she was on her way to becoming penniless. We, her three sons, jointly agreed that she should sell the house, buy a smaller more manageable flat, and use any remaining money to pay for her day-to-day living expenses. A straightforward task one might think. But no, this actually created a hell on earth for our fragmented family.

My father didn't have a bona-fide will, therefore following his death, the house officially belonged to his immediate family. My mother, and we three brothers, were not automatically assumed by the authorities to be my father's only immediate family. Mum therefore, had to put a formal notice in the newspapers to provide an opportunity for any other possible family members, to identify themselves to claim a piece of his estate. As we expected no one came forward, but in order to sell the house, Mum needed her children's formal written consent too. Under the circumstances, clearly none of us were able to go back to Iran to do this, so we had to provide our consent via post. Each of us had to have the required document approved by an Iranian Embassy. Without any exaggeration, I could write another book about the bureaucracy, ludicrous questioning and overwhelming complexity of arranging all this with the Iranian embassy in Kensington!

In order to allow Mum to sell the house, we each had to transfer and pass on our share of the estate to my mother. The identical forms required for this, which were obtained from and approved by the Iranian embassies in three different corners of the globe, were eventually hand-delivered to my mother in Tehran. Surprisingly, or perhaps unsurprisingly, the forms were found to be unacceptable, and my mother was still unable to sell. The tiny, and I mean minute foot-note on each form, stated a ridiculous and completely unrealistic house price limit.

In order to sell the house it seemed that, we three brothers, were required to visit Iran in person, facing the possible risk of prosecution, imprisonment or something worse , just for trying to sort out our fathers estate, which only involved a rundown three bedroom house (Mum's only significant remaining asset). However, something clearly had to be done to release the house from the claws of the authorities and allow it to be sold.

To cut a long story short, as they say, a property agency in Iran informed us that they'd been successful in dealing with many similar and even more complex cases, and they could easily sort out this issue without us being present. They informed us that our approved consent forms alone would suffice, and that there was no need for us to travel to Iran. We were extremely grateful and for a few days we all blindly appreciated the power behind an enhanced agency fee!

The fee was a fixed sum and not based on a percentage of the selling price. Because of this, they advised Mum to sell the house very quickly, so she agreed to sell to the first interested customer who, in all probability, I suspect had something to do with the agency.

In Iran the sale of all properties actually takes place in Real Estate Agencies called 'Mahzar-eh Moshaver-eh Amlak' in Farsi and, as far as I'm aware, without a solicitor being present.

On what was supposed to be the completion date, Mum duly visited the office (mahzar). Whilst she was waiting to sign the sale document, she noticed an unfamiliar bearded man, sitting across the room, who appeared to be giving her disapproving looks. This made her feel extremely uncomfortable. With a shaky hand she was just about to put the tip of her pen on the document, when the bearded man suddenly jumped up and announced that everyone in the *mahzar* was under the arrest.

Everyone in the office was taken to the police station. I don't know what happened to the others, but my poor mother was taken from there to Evin Prison. She was confined in a communal room along with female murderers, adulteresses, thieves, political activists and many other totally innocent individuals like her.

Bless my mother for her resilience, she found the atmosphere fascinating and found listening to the women's colourful stories about the reasons for their incarceration, even in one case, of a woman who had murdered her abusive husband, very entertaining.

She also amusingly, found most of the prison staff to be very kind and courteous and the prison food she said was excellent! Apparently the best lamb & vegetable stew with chickpeas and spices *(Ab-Ghosht)* that she'd ever had was served to her in that prison. 'Ab-Ghosht' literally means "Meat juice", and is basically a soup that is made after the ingredients are slowly stewed altogether, the dish is then strained, and the resultant clear broth is consumed with croutons or with small pieces of flatbread (*Tealit*). The remaining solid parts are then mashed up well and served in a separate dish, alongside flatbread, pickles, herb salad etc.

'Ab-Ghosht' is traditionally cooked in a stone crock pot (*Dizi*) and although it's enjoyed by all classes, it's categorised as a peasant food as it's relatively cheap to prepare (to be more economical one would just add less meat and more of the rest of the ingredients). I recall back in the 70's one could enjoy this simple but tasty dish in most ordinary teahouses or roadside cafés.

I think my mother was very lucky indeed; she was probably unaware of all the physical and psychological torture that was almost certainly going on in that prison. She was lucky too, not to have been subjected to any mistreatment, as Evin Prison was, and I understand still is, well known for its breaches of human rights and cruelty to some of its inmates, particularly political prisoners.

My mother was held there for ten days, but after paying a very handsome fine she was released. We all thought that her release was an indication of the end of her troubles, but alas this wasn't to be. A few days following her release, several heavy set official looking bearded men appeared on her doorstep and gave her only a few days' notice to clear out the house and leave! Yes, they planned to confiscate the house, officially based on her apparent wrong doing, for trying to sell her own property!

On the very day when the notice period expired, the same men, this time with official papers, appeared on her doorstep and ordered her to leave the house immediately. The neighbours' rallied round, as did some of the local shopkeepers, protesting against her eviction, but all to no avail. Mum didn't want to be physically forced out of the house, as would have undoubtedly happened, so she felt she had no choice but to follow their instructions.

She stayed with my uncle for a while, but eventually managed to find alternative accommodation in the basement of a nearby house, which belonged to a junior army officer. The basement was cold in winter and too hot in summer, and although the officer's family were respectful toward her, living in a basement like our army servants used to, especially in a junior officer's home, must have been very humiliating for the erstwhile wife of a colonel.

Within days of mum's eviction, our house became occupied by a family that apparently had lost a close member of their family in the Iran-Iraq war (1980-88). It was a gift from the government!

When the awful news of this confiscation reached me, I was very worried about my mother and immediately dialled our home telephone number. "*Alou.*" The recipient answered the call in a rough voice. "*Manzel-eh Khanoom-eh Payami?*" I enquired which means, is this Mrs Payami's home? The recipient grunted "no" and hung up. I thought I'd dialled a wrong number and redialled only to hear the same unfamiliar voice saying "No you have dialled a wrong number, this is our home and no one called Payami lives here". I was shocked and replied, "No.... you are making a serious mistake and this is not your house. It belongs to my mother. An elderly woman, a widow of a *Jenob Sarhang*, who has done nothing wrong in her life and you are daring to claim her only asset as your own." Once again the call was cut off.

I let the matter rest for a day or so, but couldn't resist phoning again. This time the wife of the man answered, "*Alou*". I introduced myself and again explained the situation. She begged me not to pester her again, saying that they too had suffered their own family misfortunes. She told me that when the government gave them the key to the house, her family knew nothing about the true circumstances. She said that now she knew all about our situation, she felt very uncomfortable and ashamed for being there.

I believed she was being genuine, and felt for her, despite the circumstances. Although my fury at the officials who'd given our home away was unabated, to her surprise, I apologised for harassing them and offered our blessing and wished them a happy and comfortable short stay, albeit as our guest!

It turned out that I'd made them feel so bad, that within a week or two they left the house and handed it back to the authorities. This turned out to be a very bad thing. The house was very soon handed to a new tenant who had a clever plan to ensure a long stay. He arranged for the house, which was on a good sized plot of land, to be converted into a day nursery.

In order to construct a row of outdoor toilets, all of the lovely mature apricot, black cherry, persimmon and medlar trees were cut down. These trees had been my father's pride and joy, along with his roses. The thought of our once beautiful garden, without the breath-taking colours of the autumn leaves and the fiery colour of the persimmon fruits, still all these years later, brings sadness into my heart. I've planted similar trees in my garden in Kent to remind me of that very garden.

I seriously considered phoning this b*****d to give him a piece of my mind, but a telephone conversation with my mother soon changed this decision. Apparently one day, my mother was passing the house and was looking at it with deep sadness, when the man suddenly rushed out , swore at her and said that if she was seen in front of the house again he would have her killed! Mum was frightened and I couldn't see that venting my, albeit entirely justified rage, would help matters. So I decided to say nothing. That I was so helpless in this situation, still preys on my mind.

It was to be many years before Mum finally got her house back. Her case sat in a huge pile of other similar cases, awaiting trial by one of the Mullahs. Finally, after yet another bribe, her case was moved to the top. Fortuitously the Mullah that heard her case was a moderate and had some sympathy for my poor mum.

She did get her house back, but didn't get any compensation, and had to face a significant depreciation in the value because of the ridiculous conversion works that had taken place. They'd ripped out the bathroom, the toilet and little of the kitchen remained. The interior was in a very poor state, and as a final insult, she was left to pay the previous occupant's utility bills! The situation left my brothers and I thoroughly frustrated.

Almost two decades of stress were beginning to take their toll on my mother's health. In that time she'd witnessed a violent political revolution, suffered discrimination by the new regime, and witnessed the persecution of her friends. She'd borne the death of her husband and found herself having to take over the management of all aspects of her life that my father had previously dealt with. She'd seen her country endure eight years of war with neighbouring Iraq, and experienced the confiscation of her home with a lengthy battle by a few corrupt individuals in authority, only to have it returned to again in a very poor state, and suffered all of this, without the support of her children.

As a final affront, during this period, Mum had been diagnosed with breast cancer, and had to have a mastectomy. She didn't tell us about this problem at the time for fear of worrying us. Mum had always been a fighter and was known by her friends and neighbours as the Lion Lady, 'Shir Zan', a title which looking back on the events of those two decades, she richly deserved.

All of these events, that were taking place back home, naturally affected me, and I worried increasingly for Mum's safety and state of health. Meantime, I was trying to adopt a European lifestyle and understand the psychology behind some people's prejudice against foreigners, especially against Iranians, since the hostage crisis in Tehran.

Persian tea (Chai)

On the right- Honey candy with pistachios & almonds (Sohan Asali)

Abghost or *Dizi*

(Traditional lamb stew with chickpeas & potato)

For 6 people

4 large lamb shanks

1 Large onion - finely chopped

1 tin of cooked chickpeas

6 medium size potatoes - peeled and cut in half

12 ladies fingers (Okra) - optional

4 tomatoes

3 cloves of garlic, peeled and chopped

2 tbsp. sour grape juice

3 dried Persian lime - soaked and poked in few places or the juice of a lime.

1 tbsp. tomato puree

1 tsp. turmeric

2 tsp. cinnamon

Salt and pepper for seasoning

A couple of bay leaves

2 tbsp. olive oil or any other pure vegetable oil

A knob of butter

1. In a large saucepan, fry the onion in oil till translucent and golden brown. Stir in the turmeric and cinnamon. Add the lamb, bay leaves and warm water to cover the meat by at least 3cm. Bring to the boil and then let it simmer on low to moderate heat. Skim off any foam as it cooks. Check occasionally and if required add more boiling water.

2. After 1¾ hours add the chickpeas, potatoes, tomato puree, sour grape juice, dried limes or the lime juice. Add more boiling water to maintain a 4cm or so of liquid above the ingredients. Mix well, season to taste and continue to simmer for a further 20 minutes.

3. Add ladies fingers if using, tomatoes and the butter and let it simmer on a low heat for a further 20 minutes till all ingredients are fully cooked and the lamb is melting off the bone.

4. Discard the bones. Strain off the broth into soup bowls and mash up the remaining solid ingredients to a pâté like consistency. Add more seasoning if necessary.

5. First enjoy the broth like a soup on its own or break up a few pieces of flat bread into it like dumplings. Wrap the mashed part in any type of flat bread with fresh herbs (*sabzi*) and enjoy like a Mexican Tortilla Roll-up. I also like to add a couple tsp. of Persian pickles (*Torshi-eh Liteh)* to each roll.

Hint:

You can also add other tinned pulses like white beans and/or kidney beans.

For my vegetarian guests, I would simply replace the meat with vegetable stock and more pulses.

Having a well brewed Persian *Chai* (Black tea, infused with a little cardamom) after all Iranian dishes, especially this one is very refreshing. However, I recommend having the chai rather weak than strong. Not too weak either, as my granddad used to occasionally complain that the "*chai passeboon dideh*" which literally means the tea has seen a policeman! (It's gone pale!).

Ghosht (Traditional Persian lamb & chickpea stew)

At least, according to Mum,

their food was tasty!

CHAPTER 14

Home Sweet Home

After successfully completing my industrial training and having been given responsibility for a large and rather complex section of the River Thames Tidal Defence Works, in addition to receiving my post-graduate qualification in Civil Engineering, I thought that finding a relevant job in the UK would be fairly straight forward.

Over the next few months, I sent out numerous copies of my CV and covering letters to various civil engineering organisations all over the country, but not one had the courtesy to short-list me. I knew this was not purely due to the recession, as my English friends had all managed to find jobs within their fields, but my equally qualified Persian friends were either unemployed or were in jobs in retail or mini-cabbing.

I didn't give up though and every month or so, for several years, I forwarded my CV without any luck. Envelopes those days were not self-adhesive, so we are talking about lots of licking and paper cuts! However I couldn't just sit and do nothing, so I made my way up the retail ladder and successfully managed a few exclusive retail units within those five years or so. The 26 year old "Trouble Maker" also managed to get a mortgage on his first flat, without any financial help from his family!

Although my basic salary in retail, together with bonuses and commission, was possibly more than the salary of a young engineer, I still however wanted to find an opening in civil engineering.

My persistence and my continued failure in finding a job with a Civil Engineering firm and the pain and disillusion this was causing did not escape the attention of an English friend of mine. One evening he asked me if he could have a look at my CV.

"Are you mad or something Mehrdad? Why on earth have you said that you're Iranian"? "Because I can't lie," I replied. "No, No, No…to non-Iranians you are not an Iranian. You're Persian! Since the revolution people tend to picture

Iranians as bearded gun toting fanatics shouting 'Death to America', 'Death to the BBC' or some such slogan! You need to distance yourself from that." "But surely the people I'm sending my CV out to are well informed and educated people, running successful businesses. Surely they're aware the word Persian is a glorified version of Iranian! " I exclaimed. "No. You'd be surprised Mehrdad. You see 'in a nutshell' people's perception of the word Persian is Omar Khayyam and his *Rubaiyat,* Persian silk carpets, fluffy cats, Shiraz wine and so on! All positive things Mehrdad."

I could see the logic of what he was saying. So I replaced only that one word on my CV, and as he recommended, included a current photograph of myself looking exactly as I would at work. The photo showed a clean shaven, gentle-looking fellow, wearing a business suit and tie.

And yes you've probably guessed correctly! Shortly thereafter I was delighted to be short-listed for the first time and yes I also got the job! My new boss had a plummy upper-class voice, and was a quintessentially British colonial, eccentric and flamboyantly, dressed in a hacking jacket and paisley bow tie. I shall refer to him as 'Mr Bow Tie'. He was one of the directors of the company and wanted very much to eliminate the racist atmosphere within his 200 or so strong organisation. I know this because surprisingly he told me so at the interview. One couldn't imagine such a thing happening today! At my interview, 'Mr Bow Tie' informed me that he would count on me as an important instrument in this endeavour. It's even more interesting to note that the director gave me only a two week trial period, despite the standard being 13 weeks!

Back in the 1980's things were significantly different and even large and reputable organisations could simply get away without having even one foreign employee. The situation now is much better, sometimes involving a quota system for the employment of minorities, although it could be argued that this in a way undermines the very idea of equality.

Around that time Mum visited me for a short period. I thought this was a good omen.

I was distressed to see her noticeably frailer than the last time I'd seen her. She'd aged twenty years in the six years since I left Iran. I was relieved and proud that I'd found myself a respectable job in my field, and was glad to be able to share this happiness and celebration with her when she arrived. However, inevitably as we caught up on the events of the past 6 years, the truth of my endless search for employment came out and I remember Mum being saddened by my tale, wishing, as mothers do, that she could have made it right for her youngest son.

On my first day at work, I turned up on the doorstep of their London Office, happy, very smart and dead on time. The office consisted of only a female secretary and eight or nine male engineers. I liked Dominic and Paul, who'd recently graduated, straight away. They were open and friendly. I ignored the less than enthusiastic handshakes from some of the older members of the team and determined to make a good impression.

My experience in retail and as a manager had taught me many useful skills, among them an ability to work under pressure and to meet targets and deadlines. I'd also honed my skills in dealing with all kinds of people, with staff both above and below me. I've always been a bit of a people person and found this came naturally to me. I'd never had a problem establishing good relations with colleagues or with customers. I was self-assured but not cocky and ready to face the new challenges ahead of me.

On the first day our group leader, after briefly introducing me to everyone, left me to sit behind a drawing table, all day and made no effort to establish what my skills were or to indeed give me anything to do. I was really bored! I was worried that I'd wasted the first day of my trial period staring at the bare walls, a green drawing table and a handful of engineers, who were head down industriously working.

The highlight of that day was my lunch break, and the occasional genuine smiles on Paul's and Dominic's faces. The group leader, who for the sake of anonymity and for obvious reasons I will call 'Mr Shaky Hands', completely ignored me, but did indulge in a curious ritual. Every couple of hours he would stand up, shake his hands about vigorously and smile to himself. I think he genuinely enjoyed doing endless structural calculations, well, each to their own! Myself I'd prefer Valium! After completing this ritual, his face would straighten, his head would go down and he'd stay there scribbling for another couple of hours or so.

The same scenario occurred the following day, and the day after that. During my first three days I kept my head below the parapet, apart from two occasions, when out of sheer boredom I asked 'Mr Shaky' to give me something to do. On both these occasions he told me that currently he had no suitable jobs for me to do.

I realised that I couldn't just sit there for my entire trial period, so I decided I would train myself with at least the latest drawings skills. I'd noticed that the engineers weren't using pencils for their drawings and instead using special pens called Isopens. So that lunch time I went out and spent my week's salary on a professional set of Isopens. Over the next three days I familiarised myself with various drawing techniques, and using these pens managed to produce a copy of an existing detailed drawing that I'd found in one of the drawers.

The Isopens staved off the boredom until the middle of the following week, but I still hadn't been given any kind of useful work. I used to go home and lie on the carpet, feeling utterly confused and demoralised. Mum couldn't understand it. Unfortunately I felt I was beginning to understand it all too well.

Having not been given a single task during my trial period, it was obvious that my days were numbered and by the end of that week they'd probably tell me thankyou and goodbye.

My flat was located on the second floor of a Victorian property with a large bay window to the front. Every day, during the final week of my trial period, my worried mum would be standing by the window looking down the street waiting for me to return home, hoping that I'd tell her that things had changed. I do recall asking whether after all this she would still invite foreigners visiting Iran for dinner or let them camp in her garden and use the family bathroom!

On Wednesday, two days before the end of my trial period, whilst all the engineers were hard at work, I was reading a manual on construction which happened to be written by one of the directors of the company. 'Mr Bow Tie' materialised right in front of my desk and asked me what I was doing. "I'm familiarising myself with the latest techniques in piling" I replied without any hesitation.

"I'm not paying £9000 a year to a graduate engineer to spend his time in the office reading and not working," he replied.

I was embarrassed and humiliated and knew all the engineers were listening, but I was prompt in replying. "I'm sorry but I'm just waiting for 'Mr Shaky Hands' to finish the design that he's working on. He wants me to draft all the necessary drawings for his scheme."

After 'Mr Bow Tie' left the room, both Dominic and Paul gave me an approving look. 'Mr Shaky Hands' was grateful that my reaction didn't land him in trouble. After that, I hoped he'd finally give me some work, but the remainder of that afternoon also passed in idleness on my part. I just couldn't comprehend why they'd bothered offering me a two week trial period, when they clearly weren't interested in me or in ascertaining my suitability for joining the group. I'd well and truly got the message.

I didn't feel like talking to anybody that night, I just wanted to go to bed and hide under my blanket, but as my mother was my guest, I had to keep my chin up and pretend that all was fine.

On the last day of my trial period, I'd had enough. The office windows were pretty dirty and obviously hadn't been cleaned for some time, so I got up, quite noisily dragged my chair to the window behind my own drawing table, climbed up and started to give the window a good clean. Imagine me amongst all those very serious engineers, in my business suit with my colour coordinated shirt and tie, standing on a chair cleaning windows!

'Mr Shaky Hands' couldn't believe what he was seeing. "What on earth are you doing Mike?" he said breaking the resultant silence of the room.

"I'm cleaning a dirty window, and I think that so far I've done a good job. Don't you think? At least I now deserve my two weeks wages from your organisation and you can justify that to 'Mr Bow Tie'. You can also inform him that for the past two weeks I haven't given any useful input into your schemes so you can jointly get rid of me this afternoon without feeling guilty about it."

He looked genuinely upset by my words. He sighed deeply and then in front of all the staff asked me what my plan was for my lunch hour. He took me to a nearby pub, and on the way there looked very uneasy and apprehensive, though he was chatting away about everything except my employment. Yes, I thought, he's just being polite and since he knows how important working for them is for me, he wants to tell me my employment is over, but somehow let me down gently. Well I was completely wrong.

He told me that from the first day he, 'Mr Bow Tie' and almost all in the office had liked my personality and thought I would fit in easily.

"So why did you and other senior engineers in the office let me suffer like that for two weeks?" I asked him bluntly.

"We've simply been very busy with a massive amount of work and I tried, perhaps not very clearly, to tell you this at least twice Mike. However your pleasant personality, good Civil Engineering drafting skills and various initiatives, especially your amusing window cleaning technique, were noted by all in this office and therefore, given the pressure we're under at the moment, there was no need to ascertain your abilities by giving you some dummy works."

Wow! This genuine, heart-warming speech took a great weight off my shoulders. He'd apparently already had a chat with 'Mr Bow Tie' and they'd jointly decided to offer me a permanent position. I promptly phoned home and the good news made my worried mother extremely happy. When I returned home, Mum welcomed me with a huge smile and a big pot of my favourite 'Saffron rice with barberries, raisins & tender chicken' (*Zereshk Polow ba morgh*).

An opening in a Civil Engineering practice, after so many agonising years of trying, was what I'd been looking for. The opportunity to get a professional job in this field and my growing experience, had created new and interesting challenges for me. This is the point in my life where I will end the first volume of my autobiography. I was finally beginning to see the light at the end of the tunnel, but many further adventures awaited me. For all I knew then, the light at the end of the tunnel could have been an oncoming train!

The word "home" has, since becoming a British Citizen, been puzzling me! Is home the place one is born and where one's childhood memories are? Or is it a foreign land which has offered security and happiness? I feel an obligation to my birth place, but somehow I often feel guilty and uncomfortable for not perhaps truly feeling that the UK is my home. It's an awkward issue and reminds me of the following humorous story.

An old man had a very long white beard. One day his friend asked him whether at bedtime he placed his beard over the blanket or under the blanket. The old man didn't answer, but a few days later his once hairy friend was beardless. "What happened to that long beard that you've been growing for years mate?" The old man replied "Ever since you asked me that stupid question of yours, I've been uncomfortable and couldn't get to sleep. I've been unhappy when my beard was placed over the blanket and equally uncomfortable if I put it under the blanket."

Finally, the poor man had no option but to shave it off! I feel similarly uncomfortable when people ask where I most feel that home is.

Mum in London – 2011

Mum in London – A year before passing away at the age of 93

Retail management time

Eventually I managed to get a job in my profession

A hands on Civil Engineer

Zereshk polo ba morgh

(Saffron rice with barberries, raisins & tender chicken)

For 6 people

For the *zereshk* chicken elements:

12 Chicken thighs or 6 chicken breast fillets plus a cup of chicken stock

2 medium sized onions, finely chopped

120g of barberries (*zereshk*) - Available in Iranian and most Turkish food stores

120g of juicy raisins

Olive or any pure vegetable oil

2 knobs of butter

1 tsp. turmeric

1 tsp. sugar

Salt & pepper

2 tbsps. Saffron liquid

For the Iranian fluffy rice

Ingredients and preparation as per *Chelow* with *Tahdig* (see Chpt.1)

1. Prepare and cook the *Chelow* with *Tahdig* as per Chpt.1

2. Meantime using a non-stick frying pan, sauté half the onions in little oil until translucent and golden brown. Transfer to a large saucepan.

3. Trim off any excess fat from the chicken portions. Wash, dry and discard any woody stems from the barberries.

4. In the same frying pan, seal the chicken for a couple of minutes on each side. If you are using chicken thighs (my favourite) fry the skin side a bit more till crispy and golden. Sprinkle over the turmeric and seasoning. After turning them around a couple of times, add them to the sautéed onions and stir. Pour over water to cover the chicken by about 2cm. If you're using chicken breast use a mixture of water and chicken stock for more flavour. Bring to the boil then simmer on a low to medium heat for 30 minutes till cooked (moist and tender). Half way through simmering add half the saffron liquid, more seasoning if desired, and if necessary top up with water or chicken stock to maintain 1cm of a liquid cover.

5. About 5 minutes or so before serving, sauté the remaining onion in little oil. Add the barberries, raisins, butter, sugar and three tablespoons of the sauce from the chicken. Cook gently for 3 minutes over a medium heat, stirring constantly, till the sauce has evaporated and the mixture has slightly caramelised.

6. Dish up the saffron rice on a platter or serve on individual plates, spread the barberry and onion mix on top and decorate with the colourful chicken pieces and *Tahdig*. Spoon over the chicken sauce and serve with *Salad-eh Shirazi* or a green salad.

Zereshk polo (Saffron rice with barberries, raisins & tender chicken)

Ah, fill the cup, what boots it to repeat.

How time is slipping underneath our Feet.

Unborn tomorrow, and dead yesterday.

Why fret about them if today be sweet!

Omar Khayyam

(Translated by: Edward Fitzgerald)

Printed in Poland
by Amazon Fulfillment
Poland Sp. z o.o., Wrocław